MW01232410

THE
END

Dr. George Madray

WinePress Publishing
MUKILTEO, WA 98275

DEDICATION

This book is dedicated to my mother, and first Sunday School teacher, Peggy McTyeire Madray.

ACKNOWLEDGEMENTS

I'd like to acknowledge the Creator and Consummator, to whom all thanks should begin and end. Through His Spirit, I have discovered many truths from the Word of God; and over the years, have adopted revelations from other inspired teachers, speakers, and authors. I believe it is our Creator who has anointed, directed, inspired, and motivated me in this writing endeavor, as well as other related opportunities, that only a short time ago I had never dreamed of.

A special thanks goes to family members, friends and others who encouraged me to write the book, and to those without whose technical help it would not have been possible.

I am also much appreciative of the technology of the OnLine Bible, which has made me appear more versed in the scriptures than I am.

ABOUT THE AUTHOR

Dr. George Madray graduated Cum Laude from the University of Georgia in 1974, with a B.S.A. degree in Agronomy (the study of the science and chemistry of soils). He then entered the Medical College of Georgia where he received his doctorate in Dental Medicine in 1977, after which he started in the private practice of Dentistry. He is involved in various business activities locally and internationally, from cosmetic manufacturing and marketing, to computer online services. He is also an inventor and holds several patents.

In 1985, Dr. Madray began to read and study the Bible seriously, with a particular emphasis on creation and prophecy. Since then, Madray has served as a part time dental missionary, and actively supports missionaries worldwide.

He resides in Brunswick, GA, with his wife, Jeanette, and their two daughters, Mariah and Bethany.

FOREWORD

Dr. Madray shows his skill in interweaving his personal interest in Creation Science with Biblical prophecy in an informative and readable account of the exciting events of the end times.

Since Creation, the Alpha moment of God, deception led to the fall of man, resulting in paradise lost. From that time onward, cataclysmic events have been shaping the world and preparing it for the grandest event in history that is yet to come.

The countdown to the day of the Lord ticks off the days, years, and millenniums of preparation for Yom Kippur, that dramatic Day of Atonement on God's calender when "Lord Jehovah, my salvation" appears as "Lord Jehovah Jesus Christ" to the Jews.[1]

The prophecies point to the end of the age of the foreign domination of Israel, which Gentiles have controlled since 606 B.C. When the full number of Gentiles has come in, Israel will have been purified in the fire of tribulation and will repent in a day (Zech. 3:9).

Dr. Madray writes that ancient Babylon will be rebuilt and from there the world economies shall be governed. The seven-year event of the tribulation is concluded by the dramatic return of the Messiah. God's Jewish remnant will see the salvation of our God, as the Anointed One in all His glory. He is seen by all as the conquering Lion of the Tribe of Judah.

From the Euphrates, four demons force the nations

---

[1] See "A Day is a Year" in Chapter Three

into a mighty thrust of destruction, which leads to Armageddon. The two hundred million demons captive under Iraq are released in a final thrust of evil (Rev. 9:14:16). Later, the Antichrist hordes opposing Israel melt away on their feet by instantaneous necrosis[2] as His glorious appearing, too terrible for words to describe, ends the war.

Messiah ultimately destroys the Antichrist by the splendor of His coming (2 Thess. 2:8). This is accomplished quickly, despite the fact that all the kings of the earth and their armies are gathered together to make war against the King of Kings and Lord of Lords. In a flash, the beast and his false prophet are thrown into Gehenna,[3] the lake of fire. The judgement—the raging fire that consumes the enemies of God—has come and the Christ of God sets up His government on David's throne to rule the world in righteousness for one thousand years (Rev. 20:4).

Upon His appearing with the hosts of Heaven, His new Kingdom will be established in Jerusalem. The cataclysmic events of His coming shake all that can be shaken. The cities crumble and the rebuilt Babylon sinks out of sight and disappears like Sodom of old. The successive kingdoms of this world—Babylonian, Medo-Persian, Grecian, Roman, and the yet future kingdoms—cease and Messiah opens His everlasting Kingdom on the throne of David, headquartered in Jerusalem where He rules from Zion (Isa. 24:23; Luke 1:32).

The destruction of this world's system, including Antichrist and his hosts, removes the evidence of fallen man. *"The wolf shall dwell with the lamb and a little child shall lead them"* (Isa. 11:6). This is the new millennium

---

[2] See "Instantaneous Necrosis" in Chapter Six.

[3] See "Great Ball of Fire" in Chapter Six.

where paradise is found again. When Messiah returns, a river shall spring forth from Jerusalem making glad the City of God, and the Dead Sea will live again (Eze. 47:8, 9).

Israel will be purified in the fire of tribulation (Isa. 66:8). All roads will lead to Jerusalem, the new world center where the Messiah will establish His Millennial rule. Former lamentations are turned into joy, war gives way to supreme peace, Jesus rules in righteousness, and mankind witnesses the eternal end of men shedding men's blood. Jerusalem, the City of our God, is clothed in His splendor; the river flowing from the City of God gives life, and the leaves of the trees are for the healing of the nations (Rev. 22:2).

Truly He has borne our sorrows and removed our transgressions so that we can see Him in all His glory as He rules in a righteous millennium in preparation for the final conflict when Jesus, the judge of the universe, casts Satan, his hosts, and the keys to death and hell into the lake of fire.

Dr. Madray does not set the day of the Lord's return—a task that only Jehovah God can perform—but reviews the course of significant historical events that have occurred on certain Jewish holy days. Underscoring the entire work is exhaustive research and thorough scriptural and scholarly documentation. From Madray's historical review, he develops a comprehensive and vivid scenario of end time events that will ultimately usher in the return of the Messiah. Then, at "the end" all will behold Him as He is, the Omega Christ of God.

George H. Meyers, Ph.D.
Executive Director
Calvary International, Jacksonville, Florida

INTRODUCTION

OVERVIEW

The big event is coming soon! The most spectacular event in human history is about to precipitate. God is preparing to lower the final curtain on the great stage of human drama—it will be THE END! As this long-awaited time approaches, God's fiery judgement and indignation will bombard planet earth with world convulsing events.

Many people, basing their beliefs on "social Darwinism" are anticipating that ever evolving mankind will create his own new world order—a utopia. With desperate but false hope, they believe life evolved from amoeba to man, and given time, man will socially evolve as well. They believe man came from ape and began to walk upright—"Homo erectus"; he then began using tools and became a handy man—"Homo habilis"; he then became wise—"Homo sapiens"; and finally, he will discover his divine nature within and become godlike—"Homo christus."

Man's imagination is one thing; God's Word is another. The Word tells us that we are inexorably moving into the most frightening time in history—the culmination of man's choice to disobey God, which began in the garden of Eden. There, everything was in perfect order, but man chose rebellion over obedience—to do things his way, and the seed of sin began to grow. The garden was truly heaven on earth, but because of sin the world has gradually become a hell on earth, and in time, truly will be.

The progressive nature of sin and its deteriorating effect on everyone, everywhere, and everything in this war zone called the world is rapidly coming to conclusion. The end times are not only clearly found in the Bible but are described in great detail.

Man first chose to disobey God, then progressively worked to remove Him completely from the world, to the point of even denying His existence. Man invented the philosophy of evolution to insulate himself by moving God further back in time and space, and hardening his conscience to God's sovereign right to rule and reign over His creation. As a result, the world is finding itself in an increasingly degenerate state and rapidly approaching the most frightening time in its history.

Divine intervention, where God, His angels, and His saints will bring an end to this evil world, is coming soon. The end is unveiled in the Bible; it is devastating as far as the world is concerned, and is so awesome that it demands one's undivided attention for its preparation.

It is the purpose of this book to move people to prepare for this inevitable end, in order to escape the coming wrath. Knowledge and understanding are prerequisite to preparation. The information in these pages covers all aspects of the end—the WHO, WHAT, WHEN, WHERE, WHY, and HOW of the end. The end will be the end of man's day of rebellion and his unbridled will. God will allow mankind a short time more before He takes over control, in what has popularly come to be known as "Doomsday." God has already laid out His plan, and has revealed it through His chosen vessel, the Jewish nation, in His prophetic word—the Bible. To understand the future, we need to understand Biblical prophecy, and what it reveals about the end.

An admonition is given in Luke 12:55 to religious people because they could not discern the signs of the times. This passage also addresses those today who, in their ignorance, choose to ignore the prophetic written Word of God. Also, in Rev. 1:3, a blessing is pronounced upon the study of prophecy. As one sees God's awesome plan of the end unfold, a cleansing and motivating effect is experienced. Once an understanding of the prophecies regarding the end times is grasped, it will separate one from the love of this world, which even now is perishing.

PROPHECY & BIBLE STUDY

The Jews have had as their historian the Holy Spirit. To Him, history is composed of past, present, and future. In His book, the Bible, He has provided—with video clarity—an overview of all time; a means by which we can zoom in and out, and replay in both reverse and forward. The Bible is the only book unique in this aspect. It gives us thousands of prophecies, of which thousands have been fulfilled. It is absolutely accurate and has been from the beginning, which testifies to its being inspired by God. Since the Bible is inspired by God, one can and should use it as the foundation for his or her belief. Within its pages, it shows us that the same One who knows the future also promises resurrection and life after death. Instruction is given on how eternal life is received (or eternal damnation), as well as how one can escape the coming wrath.

It is not just hopeless speculation when we attempt to discern the future as it relates to what God's plan and purpose is for mankind, which includes both Jews and Gentiles (non-Jews) and the Church (the mysterious union of Jews and Gentiles to God in Christ). To know God's plan, we have to gather together the many truths from the scriptures and place them in a logical and chronological sequence. This includes the periods, lengths of time, and even certain dates that God has set in prophecy for the fulfillment of His plans.

HOW TO STUDY THE BIBLE

To understand the Bible, one must take on an objective approach to what the Bible teaches. The most prevalent difficulty is not in understanding what it says, but rather in believing what it says. The majority of people strain at the truth of God's Word through the filters of their own present and past subjective emotions and experiences. These subjections, or biases, are particularly influenced by the denomination or religious sect in which the person was raised or belongs.

I once believed that the Bible was full of contradictions and problems. With so many interpretations of the Bible, it seemed proof in itself that the Bible could not be inspired. Then I began to learn more about people and more about the author of the Bible—the Creator Himself. As I realized that the One Who wrote the Bible is the same One Who created the universe, I then realized that the Bible, like the universe, must be highly organized and ingeniously inter-connected. At the same time I learned more about people, and found that they are going to believe what they want, regardless of the volume of evidence set before them. The Bible and its Author are not at fault—it's us!

The Bible is a treasure chest sent from God. In order to remove treasures from a treasure chest, the preferred method is to use a key and not a stick of dynamite. One has to be diligent and careful when studying the Bible. Second Timothy 2:15 says, *"Study to show thyself approved unto God, a workman that needeth not to be ashamed, rightly dividing the word of truth"* (KJV-King James Version). The words "rightly dividing" come from the Greek word, ortho-tomeo. It means "straight cut." As one who has practiced both in the disciplines of orthodontics and surgery, I know the value of "straightening" and "cutting." Very similar to the finesse of a surgeon, one must pay great attention to detail while "operating" on the Word of God. I dare say this is not the way most people handle the Bible; rather most tend to use it "cafeteria style" and pick and choose what they want from the surface, rather than carefully digging deeper into its limitless truths and treasures.

INTERPRETING THE BIBLE
Proper Application

First, we must interpret the Bible by understanding God's overall plan and purpose through the ages. For example, if one is to assemble a large jigsaw puzzle, he first looks at the cover of the box in which the puzzle came, which gives the proper perspective.

Second, we must discern to whom the Scriptures are addressed. For example, this doesn't mean that when there are blessings for Israel they belong to the whole Church, and when there are curses for Israel they belong only to Israel.

Third, we look at the all important context of any given portion of Scripture. A text without a context is a pretext. One must study the previous scriptures as well as the scriptures which follow. An invaluable guideline is to permit the Scriptures to interpret Scripture.

Finally, it is permissible to interpret the Bible literally. One can always spiritualize a truth away. If we over-spiritualize, then whose interpretation is right? If the literal sense makes sense, seek no other sense or you'll have nonsense!

No Contradictions

Students of the Word must keep in mind that the Bible, like the character of God Himself, will not contradict itself, and everything from Genesis to Revelation is true. False statements are accurately related as false statements. It may indeed be exactly what was said by someone who was lying, or what they truly (as an unregenerate) believed.

Following are two examples:

- Concerning the truth of man being resurrected: A demon came to Eliphaz, (during the time that Job surely must have been wondering about seeing his lost family members again), and told him *"...they perish forever"* *(Job 4:20)*. This is, according to God's Word, a lie that the demon told.
- Solomon wrote in the book of Ecclesiastes, *"For the living know that they will die, but the dead know nothing; they have no further reward..."* *(Ecc. 9:5)*. In context (see above), this is clearly a faulty statement from the human viewpoint of Solomon's frustrated observations, and not a definitive statement about life after death.

The Words of God, in tandem with His character and always true, are occasionally applied only for a certain time and as such are not to be interpreted as contradictory. For example, God prescribed in the Bible certain dietary laws. At different times man could eat only:

- plants;
- plants and any animals;
- plants and only some animals;
- and again, plants and any animals.

It appears that God may change the dietary law yet again in the future. The above changing dietary laws applied respectively to the following times:

- the time from Adam to Noah;
- from Noah to Moses;
- from Moses to the Apostle Paul;
- and from Paul to the present.

Note Language Use

As we interpret the Bible, we need to keep in mind that there are three kinds of languages—figurative, symbolic, and literal.

Following are examples:

- Figurative: *"Harden not your heart."* The meaning is clear from the context.
- Symbolic: *"In his right hand he held seven stars."* The meaning here is explained afterwards; occasionally symbolism is explained elsewhere in the Bible.
- Literal: *"Behold he cometh with clouds; and every eye shall see him."* The meaning here is that Jesus is physically coming again, and all will physically see Him.

We need to read the Bible as we would read any book, and let it say what it wants to say. There are serious consequences to misinterpreting the Bible. For example, if we spiritualize it (imagine something supplementary or non-material), the results are at least three-fold, and each becomes increasingly malignant: One, a progressive loss of truth; two, the development of conflicting denominational beliefs; and three, the creation of religious sects, or cults.

Let us keep in mind that the Bible is the only book that provides mankind with divine prophecy. Other "inspired" books such as the Oracle of Delphi, the Koran, and others, contain only man's viewpoint. Thousands of fulfilled prophecies testify to the Bible as being God's breathed inspiration. Not one single prophecy has failed. Indeed, the Bible passes the test of time!

TYPICAL PROPHECY
The Festivals

Not all prophecy is written, or stated verbatim. Some are "typical" (or prototypical), that is, a representative picture

is given of a future event. Some very interesting types of
typical prophecy are the pictures in the seven Jewish
Festivals, which are divided into two groups. The first
group (in the Spring) relate to the first coming of the
Messiah, and the second group (in the Fall) relate to His
second coming.

Much like a jigsaw puzzle, the importance of prophecy
is seen when we see that God has a clear master plan and
purpose through the ages. Since we now see that the earlier prophecies were fulfilled on specific days with Christ's
first coming; we can rest assured and have faith through
the dark times in which we live that the later prophecies
regarding His second coming will be fulfilled on specific
days as well. One can trust the accuracy of the Bible, and
the plans of God. The certainty that prophecy is God-
inspired is addressed below in 2 Peter.

Inspiration of Prophecy

*"And we have the word of the prophets made more certain,
and you will do well to pay attention to it, as to a light shining in a dark place, until the day dawns and the morning star
rises in your hearts. Above all, you must understand that no
prophecy of Scripture came about by the prophet's own interpretation. For prophecy never had its origin in the will of man,
but men spoke from God as they were carried along by the
Holy Spirit"* (2 Peter 1:19-21).

In speaking of earlier and later prophecies and their
inspiration, the book of Isaiah says:

*"I am the LORD; that is my name! I will not give my glory
to another or my praise to idols. See, the former things have
taken place, and new things I declare; before they spring into
being I announce them to you"* (Isaiah 42:8-9).

It also says:

*"Bring in [your idols] to tell us what is going to happen.
Tell us what the former things were, so that we may consider*

17

them and know their final outcome. Or declare to us the things to come, tell us what the future holds, so we may know that you are gods. Do something, whether good or bad, so that we will be dismayed and filled with fear" (Isaiah 41:22-23).

God Himself shows us above that prophecy declares divinity!

Divine prophecy contains specific details, and is both written and typical. It will be fulfilled literally and specifically by the One who has told us of the past and Who tells us of the future. The prophecies that have already come true attest to their being inspired by God. Some of the past, fulfilled prophecies show us that even the days on which the events occurred were foretold! Certainly, the future, unfulfilled prophecies concerning the end will be fulfilled as accurately!

Each chapter examines one of the following questions associated with the end—**Who, What, When, Where, Why, and How.** We are all time-bound creatures and anything as momentous as THE END will naturally raise our curiosity and interest, especially now that we see the sun beginning to set. This book was not written to satisfy passing curiosity, but to enlighten and inspire the reader, to correct and rebuke what has been improperly taught as prophecy, and to sufficiently instruct and enable others to make the decision to escape the coming wrath.

Dr. George Madray

CONTENTS

CHAPTER 1

WHO IS THE END?

Messianic Prophecies

Most end time prophecy is still future. The greatest prophecy, and the key to end time prophecy, concerns the Jewish Messiah. The Messiah is to be a human being, and at the same time equal (a fellow, or equal; see Zech. 13:7, KJV) to God. His divine nature is attested to by His being from everlasting (see Micah 5:2; Psalm 93:2, KJV). A single Old Testament passage speaks of His human nature (a child), His divine nature (a son), and addresses Him as Mighty God:

"For to us a child is born, to us a son is given, and the government will be on his shoulders. And he will be called Wonderful, Counselor, Mighty God, Everlasting Father, Prince of Peace" (Isa 9:6).

He is to reconcile man to God, necessary because of man's fall in the garden of Eden at the beginning. As we shall see, a "who" can be "an end." The question of who is the Messiah, gives us the clue in answering our question of, "Who Is The End?"

Some of the confusion over the Messiah is caused by the appearance that there were two of them. Jews began to designate them as "Messiah Ben David" and "Messiah Ben Joseph." Ben David became the conquering Messiah, and Ben Joseph became the suffering Messiah. Most Jews have only desired the Davidic Messiah, and have ignored the Josephic Messiah.

According to the prophecy of Daniel 9:25-26, the Messiah was due to arrive 69 sevens (69 x 7, or 483) after the decree to restore and rebuild Jerusalem. In order to interpret this unit of time (the sevens), e.g. seven days or seven years, we need to examine scripture.

- *"In the middle of the 'seven' he [a ruler] will put an end to sacrifice and offering"* (Dan. 9:27).
- This ruler who breaks his covenant in the middle of the seven (Dan 9:27) persecutes the Jews for 1,260 days (Rev 12:6).

Since "half" of the seven is 1,260 days, it is clear that the use of seven refers to a period of seven years (360 days in a Jewish religious year), thus the 69 sevens referred to in the decree of Daniel 9:25 is 483 years.

This decree was well known as the Edict of Artaxerxes and was given in March, 445 B.C. (Nehemiah, chapter 2). The great mistake of the Jews was that the Messiah they ignored, Messiah Ben Joseph, came but was not recognized! At the same time as Christ, about 70 others appeared, also making claim to be the Messiah. It was abundantly clear that prophecies in the Bible pointed to this time, which is the reason so many impostors showed up for their "cattle call."

Nevertheless, a suffering servant is exactly what was

predicted about the Messiah (or the Anointed One): "…the Anointed One will be cut off and will have nothing…"(Dan 9:26a). The Messiah was to suffer and die (cut off), before Jerusalem (the city) and the Temple (the sanctuary) was to be destroyed (Dan. 9:26b). Therefore, He came before Jerusalem and the Temple was destroyed in 70 A.D.

An important note is that the prophets themselves did not see that there were not two Messiahs, but two separate appearances of one Messiah. They did not divide the prophecies that foretold of His suffering from those that foretold of His glory, even though they searched the Scriptures intently (1 Pet. 1:10-12). The Old Testament prophets saw what appeared to be one mountain peak event (one coming) in the distance. Actually there are two mountain peak events (two comings) with a long valley of time (2,000 years) between them. For example, the prophet Isaiah did not see the "2,000 year comma" in the verse, "To proclaim the acceptable year of the LORD, and the day of vengeance of our God (Isa. 61:2, KJV)."

We are now living in this "comma," better known as the parenthetical dispensation of the Church Age. Therefore, Isaiah saw the prophetic and kingly work of the Messiah, but did not see his priestly work, during this 2,000 year period of the Messiah's human/physical absence from the earth. The prophets therefore saw the Altar (sacrificial suffering) and the Throne (glory), but did not see the Table (the Lord's Table). The Table represents 2,000 years of His present, heavenly, priestly work.

To the prophets and the inquiring Old Testament Jews, there seemed to be two Messiahs converging together in one distant climactic appearance. Because they rejected the notion of a separation of Messianic appearances by a single Messiah, to this day, many Jews still await their future Messiahs and the fulfillment of all Messianic prophecies.

THE TWO MESSIAHS
The Conquering King

There is much prophecy concerning the Messiah (the Christ or the Anointed One). Many of the passages appear to be contradictory, from which came the previously addressed teaching that there are two Messiahs. The first, the "Conquering King," is found in one of David's Psalms:

"The kings of the earth take their stand and the rulers gather together against the LORD and against his Anointed One [Messiah]. I have installed my King on Zion, my holy hill. You are my Son...You will rule them with an iron scepter; Kiss the Son, lest he be angry and you be destroyed in your way, for his wrath can flare up in a moment" (Psalm 2:2, 6, 7, 9, 12).

The Suffering Servant

The second Messiah, the "Suffering Servant," is found in a number of passages: *"After the sixty-two 'sevens' the Anointed One [Messiah] will be cut off and will have nothing"* (Dan. 9:26). *"He was despised and rejected by men, a man of sorrows, and familiar with suffering... He was pierced for our transgressions... the Lord has laid on him the iniquity of us all... he poured out his life unto death..."* (Isa 53:3, 5, 6, 12). (See also Psalm 22.)

Confusion by John the Baptist

The concept of two Messiahs is also demonstrated in a question by John the Baptist, who was the last of the Old Testament prophets. While it is true that John first appears in the New Testament, the early parts of the New Testament still concern the Mosaic Law of the Old Testament. What separates the physical Old Testament and New Testament is time, not the different dispensations of Law and Grace. God was just silent for 400 years!

In the last Old Testament book, Malachi, God speaks of a messenger who will come just ahead of the Messiah. In the first New Testament book, Matthew, scripture picks up the dialog where it was left off in Malachi. God announces through the angel Gabriel that His messenger would be coming to prepare the way before Him. That messenger was John the Baptist.

John had the unique position of being both a prophet and the fulfillment of prophecy. However, this prophet had trouble understanding his own prophecy! If anyone ever was in the middle of cataclysmic prophetic events, surely it was John the Baptist. Since we are so far removed from his time and it is easier for us, in hindsight, to understand past prophecy, perhaps we can also understand John's human uncertainty. John sent his disciples to ask the one called Christ (Messiah) if He was indeed the Messiah or if they should expect another (Matt. 11:3). Because it didn't appear as if Jesus was in the process of "conquering," John was beginning to question if perhaps the Rabbis of his day were right—that there were going to be two Messiahs.

From our present day vantage point, we can easily understand that instead of having two Messiahs coming at the same time and each performing different roles, we have one Messiah with two comings and two roles, 2,000 years apart. According to prophecy in Daniel 9:26, at the first coming, the Messiah is cut off (dies). Jesus' death after His first coming demands a resurrection and a leaving in order for there to be a second coming, which will occur at the end (Matt. 24:3).

As we will see, the End is associated with the second coming of the Messiah. Follow now as we step through the incredible, interconnected relationship of the Last, God Almighty, the Omega, the End, and the Messiah.

The Last Is God

Isaiah the prophet says, *"This is what the Lord says— Israel's King and Redeemer, the Lord Almighty: I am the first and I am the **last**; apart from me there is no **God**. Who then is like me? Let him proclaim it. Let him declare and lay out before me what has happened since I established my ancient people, and what is yet to come—yes, let him foretell what will come. Do not tremble, do not be afraid. Did I not proclaim this and foretell it long ago? You are my witnesses. Is there any **God** besides me? No there is no other Rock; I know not one"* (Isa. 44:6-8).

Here we see that the Last is God.

The Last Is Creator

The following is also from Isaiah, *"Listen to me, Jacob, Israel, whom I have called: I am he; I am the first and I am the **last**. My own hand laid the foundations of the earth, and my right hand spread out the heavens"* (Isa. 48:12-13).

One sees here the first and last is the Creator.

———————— ⟳ ————————

The phrase Alpha and Omega aren't used for First and Last because the Old Testament was originally written in Hebrew, and Alpha and Omega are Greek letters. The New Testament was written in Greek and we need to look there to find that phrase.

———————— ⟳ ————————

The Omega Is The Last

Alpha and Omega are the first and last letters of the Greek alphabet; thus the meaning of the many scriptural references to the first and the last. The book of Revelation states: *"...I am Alpha and **Omega**, the first and the **last**..."* (Rev 1:11, KJV). (See also Rev. 1:17, 2:8, 22:13.) The One who is the Alpha is also the Omega—He is both the Creator and the Consummator. What could make more sense than for the One who created the world to be the One who also consummates it?

The Omega is the Last.

The Omega Is God Almighty

From the book of Revelation we find, *"I am the Alpha and the **Omega**, says the Lord **God**, who is, and who was, and who is to come, the **Almighty**"* (Rev. 1:8). (See also Rev. 4:8.)

One sees here that the Lord God Almighty is the Omega.

The Omega Is The End

In Revelation 21:6, we find, *"He said to me: It is done.[4] I am the Alpha and the **Omega** the Beginning and the **End**."*

Here we see that the Omega is the End. Lastly we see, *"**Behold I am coming** soon! My reward is with me, and I will give to everyone according to what he has done. I am the Alpha and the Omega, the First and the Last, the Beginning and the End"* (Rev. 22:12, 13)." This passage explains that the Almighty God of Revelation 1:8, "who is to come," is the End.

---

[4] Part of what is "done" concerns the earth. In the past tense of this scripture, our present home was just "done" (or "done in" to use contemporary language); in other words, it is destroyed (2 Peter 3:10)!

The Omega is not only the End but is coming again at the end to reward both good and bad.

The End Is Messiah Ben David

In the 22nd chapter of Revelation, the Last, God Almighty, the Omega, the End explains, *"I am...the **End** (v. 13)"* and *"I am the Root and Offspring of **David**, and the bright and morning **star**"* (v. 16). This is the long awaited "Messiah #1," Messiah Ben David. He comes like the morning star Venus, appearing after a dark night before a new day.

The End Is Jesus

The Omega or the End—the Lord God Almighty—more specifically identifies Himself in the first half of Rev. 22:16:

*"I, **Jesus**, have sent my angel to give you this testimony for the churches."*

This star is the One who was promised in the Old Testament: "A star will come out of Jacob; a scepter will rise out of Israel (Num. 24:17)." This One who is to descend from Jacob (Jacob's Portion) is no less than the Creator: *"He who is the Portion of Jacob is not like these, for he is the Maker of all things, including the tribe of his inheritance—the LORD Almighty is his name"* (Jer. 51:19).

Again, the Messiah is human, and at the same time God. He is God's equal ("fellow" in Zech. 13:7, KJV), and of course eternal (Micah 5:2). He is one being, who makes two dramatically different appearances on the stage of human life.

God The Creator Came As A Human

First Timothy 3:14 tells us that God appeared in a body (in the flesh). John 1 explains that in the beginning (alpha) the Word made the world (Creator). He came to His own (the Jews) but they did not recognize or receive Him. In John 1:14, we see that He came in the flesh (a body) as testified to by John the Baptist. This One who is the First and the Last is also the Creator and the Lord God Almighty— about whom John the Baptist testified to being the Jewish Messiah—and who later *"poured out his life unto death"* (Isa 53:12), *"was cut off and had nothing"* (Dan 9:26)"

Who is He who died at the cross on calvary? He is none other than the Christ, the Messiah, the One who was, and who is...and the same One who is to come. He is none other than Messiah Ben Joseph!

Lord God Almighty Died And Is Alive

*"Do not be afraid. I am the First and the Last. I am the Living One; I was **dead**, and behold I am **alive** for ever and ever"* (Rev 1:17-18).

Here, part of Rev 1:8's mysterious quotation, *"who is, and who was, and who is to come"* has been explained.

The one *"who was"* means the one who existed in the past was dead (the Lord God Almighty died). Certainly, the only way for a spirit to physically die is to take on flesh, since one cannot physically harm a spiritual being. God tells us that He was pierced (Zech. 12:10), and therefore He had to have taken on a physical body.

The one *"who is"* means the one who exists in the present, who is the I AM (Exod. 3:14) or Jehovah "the existing One," who is alive forever and ever. (He is alive again and is going to stay that way.)

The one *"who is to come"* is the End. He is coming again as explained earlier, to reward everyone according to what he has done (Rev. 22:12).

SUMMARY

We can now very easily understand what the ancient prophets could not. It appeared to them that there were to be two Messiahs coming at the same time. Instead we have one Messiah and two comings. The enigma is solved when the suffering Messiah dies and is resurrected! He was Messiah Ben Joseph, the one without spot or blemish (Heb. 9:14), the sacrificial lamb (sin bearer) for those who believe (Heb. 9:28, 10:10). He is presently alive and preparing to return as Messiah Ben David, Jesus, the End, who is to be the conqueror, pouring out blood like wine and becoming king over all the earth (Rev. 19).

Depending on your relationship to Him, you could either be rejoicing in the finished work of Messiah Ben Joseph, or shaking in your boots because of the coming vengeance of Messiah Ben David, who is the Lion of the Tribe of Judah (Rev. 5:5).

Now that the question, "Who is the End? has been answered, our next question is, "What will End?"

CHAPTER 2

WHAT WILL END?

The World Never Ends

People have often spoken about the end of the world or "doomsday." Yet, the scriptures tell us that the world never ends but endures forever, *"...like the earth that he established forever"* (Psalm 78:69). Also, *"Generations come and generations go, but the earth remains forever"* (Ecc. 1:4). There will be a new earth (Rev 21:1), but the earth is changed from matter to energy—disappearing from visible sight; but in essence, it will be only a reconstitution.

END OF THE WORLD vs. END OF THE AGE

If the world never ends, then what is meant by several verses in the King James Version of the Bible that speak of the end of the world? Note especially: *"And as he sat upon the mount of Olives, the disciples came unto him privately, saying, 'Tell us, when shall these things be? and what [shall be]* *the sign of thy coming, and of the end of the world"'* (Matt. 24:3, KJV)? To this Jesus replied, *"So shall it be at the end of the world: the angels shall come forth, and sever the wicked from among the just"* (Matt. 13:49, KJV).

The word "world" in the text is largely due to the mistranslation in the King James Version of the Greek word aion. The Greek word kosmos means the external arrangement of the natural world. Aion means age. In the above passages, kosmos does not appear, but aion does. World in this case should have been translated as "age."

AN AGE DEFINED

In both science and scripture, an age is from one "cataclysmic" or "climatic" change to another in the earth's surface or condition. Thus, the age in which we now live began at the time of the flood of Noah. This is supported by evidence from both scripture and science. Scriptures tell us that before the flood the earth was quite different. Springs and artisan rivers watered the ground (Gen. 2:6, 10). There was no rain (Gen. 2:5), and the rainbow, which is formed from rain clouds, was not seen until after the flood (Gen. 9:13).

Today, we see past evidences of tectonic action in the earth's topography as exposed by the Mid-Atlantic Ridge—an underwater mountain range that has burst forth under the middle of the Atlantic Ocean, separating the world's land masses into its eastern and western hemispheres (this is particularly noticeable between Africa and South America). Flood evidence from torrents of water are located along the Mid-Atlantic Ridge and along our continental shelves. Genesis 7:11 speaks of this great bursting: *"...on that day all the springs of the great deep burst forth."* The world of that time (before the Flood) was destroyed: *"By these waters also the world of that time was deluged and destroyed"* (2 Pet. 3:6).

The Edenic Age

The entire world at the time of creation had a tropical climate and atmosphere, from the North pole to the South pole, both of which supported and sustained an abundance of life. People lived to be 900 years old. Insects and reptiles, like the dinosaurs (which got bigger and longer as they grew older), achieved great size and length. We see the evidences of that great tropical world in our present world's great fossil beds. The species of plant and animal life were abundant and varied. They, including the dinosaurs, were suddenly overcome by great volumes of catastrophic flood deposition—the flood of Noah.

Other events occurred globally as the great deep burst forth. This bursting forth produced tectonic plates in the earth's mantle. These great crustal sub-surface plates began to slide, generating massive volcanic action. This action, with the ash and super-heated water laden with minerals, caused petrification of organic material. Great tidal waves were generated, producing phenomenal destruction. The windows of heaven were opened (Gen. 7:11), bringing matter of cosmic proportions down upon the earth. Thousands of feet of flood deposition occurred all over the earth. In less than one year's time, the earth acquired its "age" (Gen 7:6; 8:13)—not over millions or billions of years as evolutionists would like us to believe.

When the end of our present age comes, the world will begin to revert back to the Edenic conditions of its earlier age. According to the prophet Isaiah, the life-sustaining power of the next age's atmosphere will be as it was before the Flood: *"Behold, I will create new heavens and a new earth. The former things will not be remembered, nor will they come to mind. Never again will there be in it an infant who lives but a few days, or an old man who does not live out his years; he who dies at a hundred will be thought a mere youth; he who fails to reach a hundred will be considered accursed"* (Isaiah 65:17, 20).

End One Age And Begin Another

The "end of the world"—or as it is more accurately translated in the New International Version of the Bible, "end of the age"—will end the present climactic conditions and begin a renewed heaven and a renewed earth. It is only logical that when one condition ends, another condition begins.

END OF PRESENT PHYSICAL ENVIRONMENT
End Harsh Atmospheric Conditions

For this new beginning to take place, this author believes there will be a physical reversal of events that happened at Noah's Flood. At the Flood, our great mountains, valleys, and oceans were formed as the great deep burst forth and the rains descended. In the coming end, these movements will be reversed—water will evaporate, mountains will sink, valleys will fill, and fountains will again be created in the process. When the earth's waters evaporate, *"the waters above the firmament"* (Gen 1:7) will be re-established. In essence, this will create a canopy of water vapor throughout the upper atmosphere. This canopy will once again produce the earth-wide greenhouse effect that was once enjoyed by the antediluvians. The canopy will capture harmful cosmic radiation, producing a pleasant, warm climate, and evenly heated surfaces on the earth from pole to pole. Such an environment will eliminate all of earth's traumatic weather conditions—blizzards, drought, hurricanes, tornadoes, and the like.

———————— ᏜᏜᏜᎾ ————————

Scientific research at Battelle Institute, in Columbus, Ohio, has shown that certain metal artifacts (a hammer) could only have come from someone who lived before the flood. This is due to the formation of a special iron oxide (Fe O) as opposed to the iron oxide (Fe_2O_3) that forms today (a much more invasive kind of rust). The only way this special iron oxide can be formed is under laboratory conditions of two atmospheres in the absence of ultra violet light. (It has also been discovered that certain rocks have trapped air pockets of 30% oxygen.) These conditions certainly seem to have been partly responsible for the longer life spans of the antediluvians (people who lived before the flood). The medical community has since proven that increased pressure and oxygen speeds the healing process.

———————— ᏜᏜᏜᎾ ————————

These waters in the high atmosphere are spoken of in God's Word as existing in the future and being established forever. *"Praise him, you highest heavens and you waters above the skies....for he commanded and they were created. He set them in place for ever and ever"* (Psalms 148:4-6). Logically, if they existed prior to the flood, are not there now, yet will be in the future, then they must be restored.

End of Volcanic Islands

The mountains and the valleys will be leveled. *"Every valley shall be raised up, every mountain and hill made low; the rough ground shall become level, the rugged places a plain"* (Isaiah 40:4). This is confirmed in Revelation

16:20: *"And every island fled away, and the mountains could not be found."*

These physical changes will restore the earth's environment to its pristine state, which will make it a much more habitable place. Both the polar ice caps and the deserts will again become fertile land, suitable for grazing and farming. The immense oceans will become narrow, shallow seas. All prominent mountains will become hills. Volcanic islands (mountains under the ocean, such as Japan and Hawaii) will sink and become smooth sea floor.

Fountains Restored

The fountains under the earth are to be reformed by the collapse of the mountains, and will help restore abundant life to the earth. *"Therefore will not we fear, though the earth be removed, and though the mountains be carried into the midst of the sea; [Though] the waters thereof roar [and] be troubled, [though] the mountains shake with the swelling thereof. Selah. [There is] a river, the streams whereof shall make glad the city of God, the holy [place] of the tabernacles of the most High"* (Psalms 46:2-4, KJV).

In chapter 47, the prophet Ezekiel saw this future river as flowing eastward into the Dead Sea, making the salt water fresh, and supporting swarms of living creatures. There will thus be an end to the famous Dead Sea that refuses to support life.

END OF THE CURSE

We have just reviewed some of the physical changes that will happen in the future, which will define the end of this age. Genesis 3:17 says the Omega will begin removing the curse of the earth that He had pronounced in the beginning (the alpha) of human history. The curse has brought to the earth what the Apostle Paul described in Romans 8 as decaying, groaning, and pain. As is well known, the curse was pronounced because of sin. Sin can be defined as man doing his own thing, which he certainly has done. Just as the antediluvians did their own thing and were awarded judgement—namely the Flood— so throughout history, people have been doing their own thing. In so doing, they are preparing themselves for judgement—the Tribulation, which leads to the end. The end is associated with the Day of Vengeance of Our God (Isa. 61:2), Who alone, after His judgement, will be able to remove the curse.

SIGN & CLOUDS

In Matthew 24:3, the Jewish disciples asked for a sign. A sign-seeker is someone who seeks a wonder or a miracle. Christ gave them the sign for the time of the end. At that time, the earth will no longer be without a sign of the physical presence of God. Therefore, signless times end.

"At that time the sign of the Son of Man will appear in the sky, and all the nations of the earth will mourn. They will see the Son of Man coming on the clouds of the sky, with power and great glory" (Matt. 24:30).

So the end comes with clouds. These clouds are like the cloud during the time of Moses' wandering 40 years in the wilderness, with a cloud by day and a flaming fire by night for guidance (Exod. 13:21). This cloud is the glory of the Lord—the Shekinah Glory (for more detail, see "Feast Of Tabernacles" in Chapter Three, "WHEN"). The Shekinah Glory will appear and stay the next time (Isa. 4:5, 6). It will be the revelation of the Lord Jesus with His heavenly entourage (2 Thess. 1:7; Jude 14).

MESSIAH'S REVELATION

The end will be the revelation of the second coming of Jesus Christ, proclaiming the Day of Vengeance. He will come the next time as a lion and not a second time as a lamb; as the Messiah Ben David, not again as Messiah Ben Joseph: *"...the Lord Almighty will come with...flames of a devouring fire...they will acknowledge the holiness of the Holy one of Jacob, and will stand in awe of the God of Israel"* (Isa. 29:6, 23).

"They will look on me, the one they have pierced, and they will mourn for him as one mourns for an only child, and grieve bitterly for him as one grieves for a firstborn son. On that day the weeping in Jerusalem will be great" (Zech. 12:10-11). (Notice the end is associated with *"that day,"* a term mentioned frequently in Scripture and equated with the Day of the Lord).

The mourning over a son that was pierced is further elucidated: *"Look, he is coming with the clouds, and every eye will see him, even those who pierced him; and all the peoples of the earth will mourn because of him"* (Rev. 1:7).

Clearly, we see that the returning Christ will be known as the One who was pierced. From Jerusalem, and around the earth, there will be great mourning because they will finally understand the mystery they have denied, that Jesus Christ always was the Savior, the God, and the Messiah of Israel!

On that great and terrible day, there will also be mourning because vengeance will be taken by the One who had come earlier to His people, *"To proclaim the year of the LORD's favor"* (Isa. 61:2). With the priceless gift of the Son of Man, God had fulfilled that prophecy before their very eyes and ears when Christ told them who He was (Luke 4:17-21). If only they had believed!

END OF NOAH-TYPE DAYS

God will pour out His wrath on mankind because of their wickedness, corruption, and unbelief—a wrath that will grow to the extent it was in the days of Noah. The disciples had asked about the end in Matt. 24:3, and Christ told them then that it would be like it was during the days of Noah.

There will be terrible times in the last days, as amplified and illustrated in 2 Timothy 3:1-4: *"People will be lovers of themselves, lovers of money, boastful, proud, abusive, disobedient to their parents, ungrateful, unholy, without love, unforgiving, slanderous, without self control, brutal, not lovers of the good, treacherous, rash, conceited, lovers of pleasure rather than lovers of God."*

It sounds as if the days of Noah are already here! When Christ was asked, *"...what will be the sign of your coming and of the end of the age"* (Matt. 24:3)? He described in detail what would happen (Matt. 24-25)—an account which outlines the book of Revelation from chapters 6 through 19. The book of Revelation was written with special attention to what is and will happen to the nation of Israel. It covers the spectrum of the end times, from the Ephesus synagogue in chapter 2, to the New Jerusalem as recorded in chapter 22. The last days of the different synagogues (churches) will be as they were during their first days.

Virtually all Bible expositors believe that all, or nearly all, the churches in Revelation chapters 2 and 3 are in the past. But with just a cursive inspection of the passages, the churches are evidently Jewish in nature, they are in, "...great tribulation" (Rev. 2:22)—and this tribulation is yet future.

TRIBULATIONS WILL LEAD TO THE END

People will suffer terrible tribulation (as clearly shown with the Churches of Smyrna and Thyatira)! Such tribulation will be unequaled from the beginning of the world, including the days of Noah, and will never again be equaled (Matt. 24:21). The things that will happen will first be God's judgement of Israel, and second God's judgement of the Gentiles (the rest of mankind). What will happen to Israel is outlined in both the Old and New Testaments of the Bible—in Daniel and Revelation.

END 490 YEARS OF SIN

God decreed 490 years for the Jews and Jerusalem to finish transgressions, to put an end to sin, to atone for wickedness, to bring in everlasting righteousness, to fulfill scriptural vision and prophecy, and to anoint the most holy (Dan 9:24). (For more detail, see "The Count Down" in Chapter 3, "WHEN.") This reconciling for sin is explained in the New Testament: *"All this is from God, who reconciled us to himself through Christ and gave us the ministry of reconciliation... Be reconciled to God... God made him who had no sin to be sin (a sin offering) for us, so that in him we might become the righteousness of God"* (2 Cor. 5:18, 20, 21).

Through the trespass of the first man, Adam (disobedient at the Garden of Eden), all were condemned. By the righteous act of the second Adam, Christ (obedient at the cross), all are offered salvation (Rom. 5:18, 19).

We can determine that 483 years of God's 490-year decree has been completed. The 483 years ended with the Anointed One (Messiah) being cut off (Dan. 9:26). After being cut off, He went back to His place (heaven) and will be there until, in their misery, the Jews earnestly seek Him (Hos. 5:15).

The seven years that remain are known as the Seventieth Week of Daniel, or the Tribulation. It is the time of Jacob's (Israel's) Trouble. An outline of what will happen in this end-time period is given in the book of Daniel: *"The end will come like a flood; War will continue until the end, and desolations have been decreed. He will confirm a covenant with many for one 'seven' but in the middle of that 'seven' he will put an end to sacrifice and offering. And one who causes desolation will place abominations on a wing of the temple until the end that is decreed is poured out on him"* (Dan. 9:26, 27). So it is that, with the Tribulation, the Lord brings an end to 490 years of unreconciled sin and its consequences.

THE ANTICHRIST

Daniel identifies the figure in the above scripture as the one from the people who would destroy the city and the sanctuary—after the Messiah had come (Dan 9:26).[5] Since Jerusalem and the Temple were destroyed in 70 A.D. by the Romans, one "from the people" would be one with Roman citizenship. This individual will be a significant "what" of the end, whose demise will coincide with the end. Since he will be the center of so many things that will take place during the Tribulation and will be such a mighty "servant" (a deliverer of judgement) of the Omega, let's look more closely at him. For our purposes, it is not possible to expound about him in as much detail as other noteworthy works.[6]

---

[5] This verse shows that the Messiah had to come before 70 A.D.

[6] The author recommends "The Antichrist" by Arthur W. Pink, Kregel Publications, Grand Rapids, Michigan.

This substantial "what" was prophesied at the very beginning of scripture (at the same time the Messiah was first prophesied), immediately after the Fall, when man and Satan first decided to disobey! The following was spoken to the serpent (the Devil): *"And I will put enmity between thee and the woman, and between thy seed and her seed, it shall bruise thy head, and thou shalt bruise his heel"* (Gen. 3:15, KJV).

This seed of the serpent will be received by the Jews as their Messiah when he appears. This person will be Satan's master deceiver on earth. In him shall dwell all the fullness of the Devil bodily. He will be the Superman who will appear according to God's prescription.

"For this reason God sends them a powerful delusion so that they will believe the lie and so that all will be condemned who have not believed the truth, but have delighted in wickedness" (2 Thess. 2:11, 12). Jesus Christ said, *"I am the way and the truth and the life. No one comes to the Father except through me"* (John 14:6).

We see why the apostle John selected the name the Anti-christ (1 John 2:18). He is The Lie, in perfect contrast to Christ, who is The Truth. God then will send the Lie, because the Truth has been rejected. Christ confirmed this: *"I have come in my Father's name, and you do not accept me; but if someone else comes in his own name, you will accept him"* (John 5:43).

The Lie, who will bring damnation, will unfortunately be well received both by Israel and the rest of the world. In fact, with the exception of Jesus Christ, he will be the most remarkable person ever to appear in human history. The Antichrist will be:

- An intellectual genius:

"...But you are a man and not a god, though you think you are wise as a god. Are you wiser than Daniel? Is no secret

hidden from you? By your wisdom and understanding you gained wealth for yourself and amassed gold and silver in your treasuries" (Ezek. 28:2-4).

Here we see that, in the future, great wealth will be obtained in a revival of the value of precious metal. As the tribulation approaches and the world economies begin collapsing, people will flock to purchase precious metals in an attempt to find security in gold and silver.

• An oratorical genius:

"The horn that looked more imposing than the others and that had eyes and a mouth that spoke boastfully" (Dan. 7:20).

"The beast I saw...had...a mouth of a lion" (Rev. 13:2).

The mouth of a lion is symbolic of an orator who gains attention and commands respect. This speaks of the majesty and awe-inspiring effects of his voice.

• A political genius:

"He will invade the kingdom when its people feel secure, and he will seize it through intrigue. After coming to an agreement with him, he will act deceitfully, and with only a few people he will rise to power" (Dan. 11:21, 23).

• A commercial genius:

"By your great skill in trading you have increased your wealth," (Ezek. 28:5).

"He also forced everyone, small and great, rich and poor, free and slave, to receive a mark on his right hand or on his forehead, so that no one could buy or sell unless he had the mark, which is the name of the beast or the number of his name" (Rev. 13:16-17).

According to Rev. 14:11, all who participate in this new "implanted" banking system will receive eternal damnation: *"And the smoke of their torment rises for ever and ever. There is no rest day or night for those who worship* the beast and his image, or for anyone who receives the mark of his name."

- A military genius:

"He will become very strong, but not by his own power. He will cause astounding devastation and will succeed in whatever he does. He will destroy the mighty men and the holy people" (Dan. 8:24).

"...they also worshipped the beast and asked, 'Who is like the beast? Who can make war against him" (Rev. 13:4)?

- An administrative genius:

"The beast I saw resembled a leopard...a bear and...a lion" (Rev. 13:2).

The Antichrist integrates the Grecian, the Medo-Persian, and the Babylonian empires. Scriptures and history show us that these animals represented these empires. The beasts are spoken of in Daniel 7:1-6, and represent the successive kingdoms in King Nebuchadnezzar's dream of the statue (Dan. 2:31). They are further identified in Daniel 2:38, 5:30-31, and 8:20-21.

"They have one purpose and will give their power and authority to the beast" (Rev. 17:13).

- A religious genius:

"He opposes and exalts himself over everything that is called God or is worshipped, and even sets himself up in God's temple, proclaiming himself to be God" (2 Thess. 2:4).

"He was given power to give breath to the image of the first beast, so that it could speak and cause all who refused to worship the image to be killed" (Rev. 13:15).

END OF THE ANTICHRIST AND 666

Good news! At the end, the Antichrist will come to his end via the laser of lasers: *"God came... His splendor was like the sunrise; rays flashed from his hand,… Sun and moon stood still in the heavens at the glint of your flying arrows, at the lightning of your flashing spear. You crushed the leader of the land of wickedness, you stripped him from head to foot"* (Hab. 3:3-4, 11, 13).

"And then the lawless one will be revealed, whom the Lord Jesus will overthrow with the breath of his mouth and destroy by the splendor of his coming" (2 Thess. 2:8).

Jesus Christ crushes this lawless one at His Revelation and fulfills Genesis 3:15, *"…he will crush your head."* At the time of the crushing of the son of Satan, those who will have received the mark and worshiped the beast or his image (Rev. 14:9) will be put to the sword (Rev. 19:21). God brings an end to the 666 system. The false prophet, and the lawless one, will be cast into the lake of fire, and Satan will be seized, bound, and thrown into the Abyss.

The above "mark" will be necessary for buying and selling, but it will undoubtably have other uses. With emerging nanotechnology, computer programers may use it to provide the genetic code information necessary to synthesize molecules and compounds to cure hereditary diseases and defects. One's passport, social security card, healthcare card, foodstamps, and transportation tokens will all be securely implanted under one's skin. It could even be used as a house key to get into one's government subsidized house. As a passport and bankcard, national boundaries will come down.

As supreme ruler, and in fulfillment of scripture, the Antichrist will say, *"By the strength of my hand I have done this, and by my wisdom, because I have understanding. I removed the boundaries of nations, I plundered their treasures; like a mighty one I subdued their kings. As one reaches into a nest, so my hand reached for the wealth of the nations; as men gather abandoned eggs, so I gathered all the* countries; not one flapped a wing, or opened its mouth to chirp'" (Isa. 10:13-14).

The "mark" and its system that promised benefits such as convience, identification, security, etc. will instead become enslaving, demanding, monopolistic, and predatory. In this diabolical, encompassing, economic, political, and religious system, the governor becomes god. And like good dogs, the ones provided for will worship the provider.

Syringe-implantable identification transponder biochips utilizing low frequency FM radio waves are already in use in animals. Perhaps a biochip will be the mark, efficiently tying each recipient into the Antichrist's global computer system. What else but computers would be associated with a world-wide system of alphanumerics (numbers and letters).

For those who come to faith between the pre-tribulation rapture and the mid-tribulation rapture (for explanation of these events, see "The Festivals" in Chapter Three), the Lord has given a way to figure out who the Antichrist will be—by calculating his number. With this foreknowledge they will be forewarned and able to make preparation. God tells them that the Antichrist's number is 666 (Rev. 13:18). Perhaps the mystery will be solved through gematria, explained by Salem Kirban in the Salem Kirban Reference Bible (AMB Publishers, Chattanooga, TN ©1992, pg. 220):

"Gematria was the ancient system of number coding and of spelling out numbers by letters. Any alphabet can be used. The code uniformity runs like this, here using English: a=1; b=2; ....; j=10; k=20; ...; s=100; t=200; ...; etc. Thus the name "fox" would yield 6+60+600 or 666."

END OF THE TRIBULATION

With the destruction of the Antichrist and his armies, the Seventieth Week of Daniel, or the Tribulation, will come to an end. Moreover, with the end of the Tribulation, the purification process of Israel ends as well, as described in Daniel 9:24: (paraphrase): *"Transgression is finished. Their sin is put to an end; it is reconciled for, everlasting righteousness is brought in; vision and prophecy is fulfilled; and the most holy anointed* (the anointed one, or Christ) *is anointed king."*

So Earthly kingdoms will end, along with the Tribulation.

"In the time of those kings, the God of heaven will set up a kingdom that will never be destroyed, nor will it be left to another people. It will crush all those kingdoms but it will itself endure forever" (Dan. 2:44).

END OF THE TIMES OF THE GENTILES

Along with the end of the Antichrist, the tribulation, and the purification of the Jews, the time of the Gentiles also comes to an end. Their existence began in 606 B.C. when, after the Jews fell into idolatry, King Nebuchadnezzar of Babylon carried them into a 70-year captivity. Since then, God has permitted the Gentiles to have world power, as outlined in Daniel 2:37-43.

Christ remarked about these times: *"Jerusalem will be trampled on by the Gentiles until the times of the Gentiles are fulfilled"* (Luke 21:24).

THE DAY OF THE LORD
The End Day + 1000 Years

This last or end day is known in scripture as "That

Day." It is also known as the Last Day, the Great Day, and the Day of the Lord, among other names. The Day of the Lord begins after the multitudes gather (for the Battle of Armageddon) in the valley of decision; and at the time that the sun and moon are darkened (Joel 3:14-15). At the time the sun and moon are darkened, the Son of Man (the Messiah or Christ) comes in great glory (Matt. 24:29-30). Therefore, the Day of the Lord (That Day) begins at Christ's return. This end "day," or Day of the Lord, is 1,000 years in duration. At its beginning it ends this present age; at its end, it ends the Millennial Age or Day; consequently ending two ages. The future end (1,000 years plus) is spoken of by Peter, *"But the day of the Lord will come as a thief in the night; in which the heavens shall pass away with a great noise, and the elements shall melt with fervent heat, the earth also and the works that are therein shall be burned up"* (2 Pet. 3:10, KJV).

We who have studied physics, and many others, see these "elements melting" as atomic fission.[7] Elemental matter (the earth and its atmosphere) is converted into energy, and disappears—releasing "fervent" heat. This elemental disappearance of the earth after the 1,000-year Day is yet a different end. Its destructive end leads to judgement for those in Hades, who did not bow their knee to God while they were alive (Isa. 45:23). These damned ones under the earth will bow their knees before God/Christ (Phil. 2:10), and will be judged after the earth disappears—at which time they are exposed and resurrected in preparation for the "second death," which is

---

[7] Nuclear fission is a reaction in which an atomic nucleus splits into fragments, usually two fragments of comparable mass, with the evolution of approximately 100 million to several hundred million electron volts of energy. (American Heritage Dictionary.)

explicitly described in scripture: *"...all they that go down to the dust shall bow before him: and none can keep alive his own soul"* (Psalm 22:29, KJV).

"And when the thousand years are expired...the devil that deceived them was cast into the lake of fire and brimstone, where the beast and the false prophet are... And I saw a great white throne, and him that sat on it, from whose face the earth and the heaven fled away; and there was found no place for them...and hell delivered up the dead...and they were judged according to their works. And whosoever was not found written in the book of life was cast into the lake of fire... This is the second death" (Rev. 20:7, 10, 11, 13, 15, 14 KJV).

The "second death" is when death, hell, sin, unrepentant sinners, and Satan find their end. Only then can God lift the curse He pronounced at the beginning, after mankind fell in the garden of Eden. Humanity has come full cycle; we are back to the very beginning: *"In the beginning God created the heavens and the earth"* (Gen. 1:1).

In this new beginning God has prepared, *"a new heaven and a new earth, for the first heaven and the first earth had passed away..."* (Rev. 21:1). He will have purged the rebellious men and angels, and a perfect earth is possible once again, this time without the existence or presence of sin and evil.

SATAN'S & MAN'S 6,000 YEAR "WEEK" ENDS

The end at the beginning of the Day of the Lord (a 1,000 year "day") will end man's week. (Man will have had approximately six 1,000-year "days" since the garden of Eden, as calculated by tracing the genealogies in the Bible from Adam to Christ and through the present). God will then regain control. The book of Revelation expounds many details of God's "take-over." God takes back the title deed to the earth that He gave to Adam, who in turn gave it to Satan at the Fall. God gets the deed back from Satan (the god of this age, 2 Cor. 4:4) by unrolling the seven sealed scroll of Revelation. By God's decree, man will no longer have to suffer under the curse, or pay the price for being painfully educated by the tree of the knowledge of good and evil (Gen. 2:17).

Seven Seals

Seven seals in the book of Revelation outline the entire period of tribulation. Inexplicably, the sixth seal seems to be at the very end, for the events that coincide with its "opening" appear to be the same events that take place at the end of the tribulation: The sun turns black, the moon turns red, the stars fall, the sky recedes, the mountains move, and men hide (Rev. 6:12-16). Yet the sixth seal is opened before the seventh seal, which contains the seventh trumpet, heralding the end time events that bring in the Day of the Lord. This presents an enigma. How can we have the Day of the Lord both at the middle of the tribulation and at its end? As shown above, the Day of the Lord begins after the multitudes are gathered in the valley of decision, to await the Battle of Armageddon (Joel 3:14).

One plausible answer is that there is a proclamation at the middle of the tribulation, a warning if you will, that has some of the same signs as the Day of the Lord. The prophet Zephaniah associates a voice with the Day of the Lord, which could be a type of preceding proclamation:

"The great day of the Lord is near, it is near, and haseth greatly, even the voice of the day of the Lord: the mighty man shall cry there bitterly" (Zeph. 1:14 KJV).

This voice then, preluding the Day of the Lord, apparently acts as a warning three and one-half years before the actual event. It is at the sixth seal (not the end, or day of the Lord) that people will say to the mountains, "*Cover us*" and to the hills, "*Fall on us*" (Hos. 10:8; Luke 23:28-30; Rev. 6:16).

Seven Trumpets

Within the seventh seal are seven trumpets, four of which are trumpet plagues that bring to an end the following: 1/3 of the trees and grass; 1/3 of the sea (with its ships and sea creatures); 1/3 of the drinking water; and temporarily dims 1/3 of the energy output from the sun, moon, and stars.

After these four "warnings" come the remaining three trumpets, known as woe judgements. A visible, flying angel announces three supernatural woe judgements, which soon follow. The fifth trumpet inflicts tormenting "locusts." The sixth trumpet releases 200 million "horsemen," killing 1/3 of humanity. The seventh and last trumpet is composed of seven bowls of wrath.

Seven Bowls Of Wrath

The seven bowls are seven supernatural plagues. The first bowl produces sores on those who accepted the mark of the beast. The second turns all the oceans into blood, killing all sea creatures. The third turns the rivers and springs that are used for drinking water into blood. The fourth causes the sun to scorch humanity with great heat. The fifth plunges the Beast's seat of government (Babylon) into darkness. The sixth dries up the Euphrates River and releases demons to gather the world's armies to Armageddon. The seventh produces the incomprehensible earthquake that tumbles all major cities (with their "indestructible" skyscrapers)—and also produces great hailstones, which cause the future city of Babylon (in present day Iraq) to go to meet the earlier sin-consumed cities of Sodom and Gomorrah. It goes down into the earth and is covered by the sea (Jer. 51:42, 64; Rev. 18:17-21).

Numerous Other Ends

Throughout Scripture are prophecies of yet more ends. The wicked and their cities come to and end (Ps 9:5,6); the sadness of the earth ends (1 Chr. 16:31-33); wars end (Ps 46:9); and the carefree life of the wicked, along with their increase in wealth ends (Ps 73:12,18). The physical bodies or ashes of the righteous multitude, which are in the graves of the earth end (Dan. 12:2; Isa. 26:19; Hosea 13:14); the frustration of the earth with its bondage and decay ends (Rom. 8:20,21); and perhaps the division of languages, which was instituted at the Tower of Babel, ends (Zep. 3:9).

Satan, the god of this age, blinds the minds of unbelievers so they don't see the glory of Christ, who is the image of God (2 Cor. 4:4). So, along with Satan's end (Rev. 20:2), there will be an end to all the blindness that he has perpetrated. The flogging, impoverishing, imprisonment, mistreating, ridiculing, robbing, squelching, torturing—and killing—of the faithful will end forever (Heb. 11:35-38). Amen and amen!

Lord's Prayer Will End

All the way to the end of time, the faithful will have been praying what has been historically known as the Lord's Prayer. Their petitions—for God's kingdom to come; for His will to be done on earth as it is in heaven; for daily bread (including supernatural manna, Isa.

33:16); for not being led into temptation (the testing of the tribulation); and for deliverance from the evil one (the Antichrist, Matt. 6:9-13)—will all be answered on the day of the Lord! As of that glorious day, the Lord's Prayer will no longer need to be prayed by any of God's saints.

Evildoers End

The Lord will bring an end to Nineveh (present day Mosul, Iraq), and some of her descendants who were born there, such as the Antichrist (Nah. 1:11, 14).[8]

The whole seventh chapter of Ezekiel speaks about The End. At the end, God's anger is unleashed. One can see in this chapter things that will happen throughout the tribulation as well as at the end. These are the same events that are detailed in the book of Revelation.

The end brings separation of the sheep and the goats (figuratively, the good and the evil). These are the people who make it through the tribulation period alive and are on the earth when God reveals Himself (Zech. 12:10). The evil are separated (as they were in Noah's day): *"Two men will be in the field; one will be taken and the other left"* (Matt. 24:40). Jesus will first put the evildoers on His left side (Matt. 25:33), and then into eternal fire (Matt. 25:41).

Man's System Ends

Man's week in the sun ends; his politics centered at Rome, his religion centered at Israel, and his commerce

---

[8] Nahum speaks of one who has come forth from Ninevah who plots evil. It is unlikely that this verse is referring to King Sennacherib (King of Assyria), a type of the Antichrist, for the Day of the Lord (the End) is in view here. See verses 2, 5, 12, and 15.

centered at Babylon, all come to a prophesied end. Man's new "miraculous" world order, created by the illustrious and charismatic Antichrist, crashes like a lead balloon!

SUMMARY

Also terminated at the end is the fragmentation and division of believers within the Church. Finally, the end brings the bodily resurrection of the righteous, and with this glorious day an end to the long separation between God's living elect and all who died in Christ.

As stated previously, the world is never completely destroyed, but it is only the age in which we now live that will definitely come to an end. Our present higher mountain ranges and volcanic islands will disappear, giving us a radical change in climate worldwide. Satan's reign of authority over the people of the earth, epitomized in the Antichrist, will end. The seed of the woman, Christ, will crush the seed of the serpent, Antichrist (Gen. 3:15).

One thousand years after the end of this age (after the 1,000 year Day of the Lord), the earth as it now appears will disappear in an elemental level reconstitution, and a new heaven and a new earth will be formed. The earth will be reconstituted to its original perfection, and man will become immortal. Both earth and mankind will have come full circle, returning to their pristine, original state of existence. Once again, being made in the flawless image of God, man will live forever in an Edenic environment with his Creator.

With all this simultaneous good and bad news, we naturally seek to know when all these things will take place. "WHEN" is the subject of the next chapter.

CHAPTER 3

WHEN IS THE END?

That Day, the End Day, Is Restoration Day

While anyone can, and so many have set actual dates, the only dates that could count are dates that God would have set. Has He set dates? Where and how can we find them and interpret them, particularly "That Day"—the End Day, the Day of the Lord?

The disciples of Christ asked Him when the age would end (Matt. 24:3). In essence, they asked Him about the Day of the Lord.

Christ remarked, *"No one knows about that day or hour, not even the angels in heaven, **nor the Son**, but only the Father"* (Matt. 24:36; Mark 13:32).

In the first chapter of Acts, we see the disciples of Christ asking Him again, after His resurrection, about that day. Several things are shown in scripture. We must remember that by that time, Christ had reclaimed the glory He had before the world began (John 17:5); the same glory He now shares with the Father in heaven (1 Tim. 3:16), with all wisdom and knowledge (Col. 2:3).

Christ tells them again that it was not for them to know the times or dates the Father had set (Acts 1:7). However, at this time, He did not say that He (the Son) did not know the date. At this second asking, Jesus did not claim not to have this knowledge because He was then omniscient, once again!

The above passage (Matt. 24:36) was certainly true while Christ appeared in human flesh, but it did not pertain to Christ in His post-resurrection/glorified state, approximately forty days later, nor does it pertain to all people future to the time that it was stated. It is axiomatic, that all will know when it is all over. The words translated there as "no one knows" do not mean "no one will know." Actually, the word in the Greek is eido, which is used in the perfect tense and describes an action which is viewed as past tense. Accordingly, it should be translated as it is in the YLT (Young's Literal Translation) as "no one hath known." No one having known before Christ's resurrection in any way precludes everyone from knowing later. Therefore, let us not stumble over one passage, but continue to seek from the prophetic word of God.

The disciples equalled that day, the end day, with the time of restoring the kingdom to Israel (Matt. 24:3; Acts 1:6). This is also seen in the Old Testament (Amos 9:11; Dan. 2:44). These passages clearly equate the end with the restoration of Israel. If we can find out when the restoration will take place, then we will know when the end will be.

THE BIBLE SETS DATES

The Book of Revelation was written decades after the books of Matthew and Mark. Once certain events of the tribulation take place, one can know when other events, and when the end will occur! Once the abomination is set up that causes desolation (Dan. 12:11), it will lead directly to the end of this age. According to Daniel 12:7, this is to be for a time, times, and a half a time, or 3-1/2 years.

When Christ spoke of the end, He remarked that there would be an abomination in the Temple (which has to be rebuilt), and that it would cause desolation. This is the same thing spoken of by Daniel. Christ instructed the people to flee the area because the greatest of tribulations would begin (Matt. 24:15-16, 21). The people who flee (to a specially prepared place) will be taken care of for 1,260 days (Rev. 12:6).

We now see that the end will come 1,260 days from the abomination. Therefore, once this abomination is seen, anyone can begin to put an "X" through each successive day on a calendar, and do this exactly 1,260 times, until the Lord of Glory appears at the Revelation.

Dates/Signs Are For The Jews

God has clearly given signs to His sign-needy people, the Jews. *"Jews demand miraculous signs..."* (1 Cor 1:22). But, as the Apostle Paul instructed the Church, *"We live by faith, not by sight"* (2 Cor 5:7). The Messiah remarked, *"A wicked and adulterous generation looks for a miraculous sign..."* (Matt. 16:4).

As time passes, evil grows. After the Church is raptured (the translation of true believers to heaven), evil will no longer be restrained (2 Thess. 2:7). All who are left on the earth at that moment are evil. Among this wicked generation, God will once again provide signs, and again, He will deal predominately with the Jews.

Once again, signs will accompany God's message and messengers.

To understand more about signs and times, and to distinguish them from what is signless and timeless, we need to examine the difference between prophecy and mystery.

Prophecy vs. Mystery

The early Church, mostly Jewish, was living in expectation of the coming Kingdom of Israel—thus they are known as the "Kingdom Church." Not all of the Jews repented as Peter had instructed them to do (Acts 2:38). Miraculous signs and wonders continued, and Peter again instructed them to repent and to receive the times of refreshing, with its revelation of Jesus Christ (Acts 3:19-21).[9]

This "Kingdom Church" was looking for the revelation of Christ onto the earth. By Acts 28, the Jews' heart had become calloused and God's salvation was sent to the Gentiles (Acts 28:27-29). This great responsibility was given to Paul (Eph. 3:1-2). He spoke of the Jews rejection of the Gospel and how he was the apostle to the Gentiles, to make the Jews envious (Rom. 11:11-18). The new and distinct body of believers formed through Paul is known as the "Mystery Church." It is also known as the Church of Grace because of its emphasis on the gospel of God's grace (Acts 20:24).[10]

---

[9] Here we have restoration coming at the time of Christ. As we saw in great detail in the previous chapters of this book, the end occurs at the revelation of the End Himself. Again, the end will occur and restoration will begin, all on that day when Christ is revealed.

[10] For further study, the author recommends, "Studies in Dispensational Relationships" by Charles F. Baker, Grace Publications,Inc., Grand Rapids, Michigan.

The early Church—the prophesied, or Kingdom Church—emphasized the gospel of the Kingdom. It proclaimed that the kingdom of heaven was near, that it began with John the Baptist (Matt. 3:2), continued with Christ (Mark 1:15), and later with others (Luke 10:1; Matt. 28:19). It is the gospel of the Kingdom that will be preached again in the future by 144,000 Jews (Rev. 7; Rev. 14), as well as by the prophet Elijah. It will be preached after the Mystery Church is raptured: *"...in the whole world as a testimony to all nations, and then the end will come"* (Matt. 24:14). The Kingdom Church will be looking for the Revelation of Jesus Christ onto the earth. The Mystery Church is looking for the Rapture—meeting Jesus Christ in the clouds in the air (1 Thess. 4:17).

The present church—the non-prophesied, or Mystery Church—emphasizes the gospel of the grace of God. It says that those who accept the death of Christ on the cross as their sacrifice for their sins, and believe in His resurrection from the dead, will have eternal life (Rom. 10:9).

The message of Bible prophecy has been cursed by people who do not know that we are in the Mystery Church and, by believing that we are in the Kingdom Church, have set dates for the Rapture, which is signless and timeless—as if it were the Revelation, which has a prophesied, definite, sign and time! (For more details, see "The Mystery" later in this chapter.)

Unlike the rapture, the end day, defined by the Revelation of Jesus Christ onto the earth at the Mount of Olives, can be calculated with close precision. In Matthew and Mark's day, no one had known "the day or hour" of the Revelation (Matt. 24:36; Mark 13:32). This doesn't mean that decades later when the book of Revelation was unveiled, that people would forever be in a dark veil about the date of Christ's Revelation.

"People saved during the early part of the Tribulation will have opportunity to study the Scriptures, hear the teaching of the 144,000 (Rev. 7) and *exactly calculate the day Jesus will set foot on the Mount of Olives.* For, from the time of the abomination of the future temple by the Antichrist (Matt. 24:15-22; Mark 13:14; 2 Thess. 2:3-4; Dan. 9:24-27; 11:31; and 12:11), it will be exactly 1,260 days until Jesus fulfills Zechariah 14:4 when He sets foot on the Mount of Olives on the East of Jerusalem."[11]

It is certainly more difficult to find the time of the Revelation of Christ the further the event is from the present. Unlike the Rapture, the Revelation is a subject of Old Testament prophecy. We would then expect to be able to glean information, however veiled, which would shed light on the subject. Let's look!

Remember, the end day is comprised of several events that are all associated with restoring the kingdom to Israel. In the previous chapter, we saw different events of the end day: the end of Man's Week; the end of Gentile kingdoms; the destruction of the "prince," associated with the abomination which will have caused desolation, and the Revelation of God—better known as Jesus Christ, all occur at that "end day."

Since we understand that the "end day" (that day) is concurrent with restoring the kingdom to Israel, we need to examine any prophecies related to "that day"—that Day of the Lord, with its wrath and restoration—in order to determine when it will occur.

---

[11] David Allen Lewis, The Triumphant Return of Christ, Green Forest, AR: New Leaf Press, 1993, pg. 333.

WRATH AND RESTORATION

Some verses in the Bible that relate to wrath, and then to restoration, are the closing verses of Hosea, chapter 5, and the beginning verses of Hosea, chapter 6. There also, we are given a date set by God!

"Then I will go back to my place until they admit their guilt. And they will seek my face; in their misery they will earnestly seek me. Come, let us return to the Lord. He has torn us to pieces but he will heal us; he has injured us but he will bind up our wounds. After two days he will revive us; on the third day he will restore us, that we may live in his presence" (Hosea 5:15; 6:1,2).

The date is, *"on the third day."*

In the context of this passage, if we read the verses just before this, the Lord is speaking judgement upon the Northern Kingdom (Ephraim), which would be quick; and on the Southern Kingdom (Judah), which would be slow (moth vs. rot, Hosea 5:12). This certainly speaks of the times of the Assyrian King and later the Babylonian King several centuries before Christ. But as we will see in the next section, it speaks of God—in the person of Christ—going back to His place.

Israel had strayed and rebelled against God (Hos. 7:13). For doing so, certain prophesied consequences would (or will) occur: God would, *"...turn away from them"* (Hos. 9:12); there would be, *"...wombs that miscarry and breasts that are dry"* (Hos. 9:14); the Jews would be, *"...wanderers among the nations"* (Hos. 9:17) ; and they would, *"...have no king..."* (Hos. 10:3). At the end, *"...they will say to the mountains, 'Cover us!' and to the hills, 'Fall on us'"* (Hos. 10:8)! Nations will gather against them (Hos. 10:10); and they will finally seek the Lord, Who will come again to Israel (Hos. 10:12). This "coming again to Israel" refers to that day—the end day.

The history of the Jews since their rejection of God (in the person of Jesus the Messiah at the cross, or Messiah Ben Joseph), has been one of misery. As He was being led to the cross, Jesus reminded them of His words from the prophet Hosea:

"Daughters of Jerusalem, do not weep for me; weep for yourselves and for your children. For the time will come when you will say, 'Blessed are the barren women, the wombs that never bore and the breasts that never nursed!' Then they will say to the mountains, 'Fall on us!' and to the hills, 'Cover us'" (Luke 23:28-30)!

Only forty years after Christ's statement, the Jews were sent to wandering, and have not had a king since. All the other events spoken above in Hosea 10:8-12 will occur at the end. Hosea also tells us about what will happen in the Tribulation.

Hosea 13:7-8 speaks of a lion, a leopard, a bear, and a wild animal (a beast). This parallels the Gentile kingdoms that have ruled and will rule over Israel until the Lord returns. It also represents the future tribulation of the woman with the pains of childbirth (Hos. 13:13). These same animals—the lion, the leopard, the bear, and the wild beast will be represented in the soon coming ruler— the Antichrist—the one spoken of in the Old Testament as being the Assyrian (Micah 5:6). He will be a composite of the beasts that Daniel saw. The last "wild animal" is a composite beast, and is mentioned in Rev 13:2. It will be a revived combination of the old Roman empire, and the Babylonian, Assyrian, and Grecian empires as well. Its ruler, the Antichrist, will rule the territory of the old Roman empire—north, south, and east of the Mediterranean Sea.

This won't be merely the European Union or the European Economic Community, as so many contemporary

Bible prophecy teachers postulate. This is wrong because Europe's geographic location alone does not fit the facts (see the section, "Babylon" in the next chapter), and because the ten kingdoms with their ten kings aren't established until the Antichrist is a king (Rev. 17:12), which is after the Tribulation starts.

GOD LEAVES ISRAEL

Since we see that Hosea speaks not only of his time but a far distant time, we can apply the prophecies of Hosea (5:14-15; 6:1-3) to a time much further in the future.

In Hosea 5:14-15, God said, *"I will tear them to pieces and go away... I will go back to my place until they admit their guilt."*

In Matthew 23, Christ mourns, *"O Jerusalem, Jerusalem, you who kill the prophets and stone those sent to you, how often I have longed to gather your children together, as a hen gathers her chicks under her wings, but you were not willing. Look, your house is left to you desolate. For I tell you, you will not see me again until you say, 'Blessed is he who comes in the name of the Lord'"* (Matt. 23:37-39).

He also said about the temple building, *"I tell you the truth, not one stone here will be left on another; every one will be thrown down"* (Matt. 24:2). Christ spoke these words in 30 A.D., and the temple was destroyed in 70 A.D.

On the cross, Jesus said, *"Father, forgive them, for they do not know what they are doing"* (Luke 23:34). The Father answered the Son's prayer, and judgement was not brought immediately, but was postponed forty years.

The number 40 is God's number of probation. Moses was on probation 40 years in Egypt, 40 years in the desert, and 40 years (along with Israel) in the wilderness. The reigns of Saul, David, and Solomon each lasted 40 years. Nineveh was given 40 days to repent. Christ was tested 40 days by Satan, and was with his disciples after his resurrection for 40 days.

We can now establish the time when God, in the person of Christ, went back to His place and hid His face (Hosea 5:15); also in Hosea 5:15, and Matthew 23:39, when He promised that the Jews would not see him again until..... The time when God left was 30 A.D., when He was crucified.

The place spoken of is none other than the New Jerusalem—heaven. *"In my Father's house are many rooms... I am going there to prepare a place for you. And if I go and prepare a place for you, I will come back and take you to be with me that you also may be where I am"* (John 14:2-3).

This is the place where God/Christ dwells—The Father tells the Son, *"The LORD says to my Lord: `Sit at my right hand until I make your enemies a footstool for your feet'"*(Psalm 110:1). To the Son he also says, *"Your throne, O God, will last for ever and ever... Sit at my right hand until I make your enemies a footstool for your feet"* (Heb. 1:3,13).[12]

We see here that God's/Christ's place is in heaven, to which Christ ascended, and from which He has promised to return.

---

[12] Note here that the Father Himself shows us that the Son, Christ, is God.

ISRAEL'S RETURN TO THE LORD

Next, we need to examine the passage in Hosea 6:1 that speaks of Israel's return to the Lord for healing, to see when it applies: *"Come, let us return to the Lord. He has torn us to pieces but he will heal us; he has injured us but he will bind up our wounds"* (Hosea 6:1).

The book of Jeremiah shows us that the time of this return, was not, as many believe, when Israel became a nation in 1948. *"'Return, faithless Israel,' declares the LORD, 'I will frown on you no longer, for I am merciful,' declares the LORD, 'I will not be angry forever. Only acknowledge your guilt...' declares the Lord"* (Jer. 3:12-13).

"At that time they will call Jerusalem, The Throne of the LORD, and all nations will gather in Jerusalem to honor the name of the Lord. No longer will they follow the stubbornness of their evil hearts. In those days the house of Judah will join the house of Israel..." (Jer. 3:17-18).

The time spoken of for this return is after the future 70th week of Jacob's trouble (The Tribulation). "At that time" and "in those days" will be during the Day of the Lord, when Israel is to be restored—after the end. The nations of the world will be gathering in Jerusalem to honor the name of the Lord. That time of restoration certainly is not going on as of this writing!

HOSEA 6:2—LORD IS AWAY TWO DAYS

This next verse gives us the length of time that God will be away before the restoration, which as we have seen begins at the end: *"After two days he will revive us; on the third day he will restore us, that we may live in his presence"* (Hos. 6:2).

Let's really dissect this passage! The word *after* is not

very specific at all when you think about it, for everything comes after something. One wonders why it would even be there in such a specific time passage as this. Using the word *after* implies that it could be any time after two days, or any time in the third day rather than "on the third day" (at the beginning of the third day).

The reference to this passage in Strong's Exhaustive Concordance of the Bible, shows that the word *after* has no corresponding reference number behind it. According to the instructions in Dr. Strong's book, this means that the word does not appear in the Hebrew text of Scripture; that it was added by the translators for clarity. So we can drop the word *after,* because it has been added.

Revival And Restoration

The next key words in the passage are revive and restore. Revive also appears as the translation in the King James Version (KJV). It means to quicken—and the Lord is certainly going to be doing this during the Tribulation. In the KJV, restore is translated raise up. It means to be established, as well as to raise up or restore. The Lord has certainly made it clear that Israel will be restored at that day (the day of the Lord): "In that day I will restore David's fallen tent (Amos 9:11)."

Chapters 8-13 of Hosea further expand the Hosea 6:2 passage on reviving. It is clear that this will occur in the future. For they, *"...begin to waste away under the oppression of the mighty king"* (Hos. 8:10)." This, of course, is the Antichrist. *"The days of punishment are coming"* (Hos 9:7), refers to the last week of Daniel's 70th week, or the Tribulation.

All is stated clearly in Hosea 3:4-5: *"For the Israelites*

will live many days without king or prince, without sacrifice or sacred stones, without ephod or idol. Afterward the Israelites will return and seek the Lord their God and David their king. They will come trembling to the LORD and to his blessings in the last days."

The first sentence refers to their present kingless state; the second, of their restoration. The Israelites will be purged of their dross and then restored as they were in days of old (Isa. 1:25,26). Zephaniah, who speaks of the day of the Lord (Zeph. 1:14), promises, *"At that time I will gather you... when I restore your fortunes before your very eyes,' says the Lord"* (Zeph. 3:20). Jeremiah 16 also speaks of the latter days, and refers to the combination of wrath, followed by restoration.

The Scriptures associate this day of the Lord ("that day") with rest: *"In that day...his place of rest will be glorious"* (Isa 11:10). In the 3rd chapter of Acts, the Apostle Peter explains to the men of Israel that they had killed the author of life, but that God had raised him from the dead. He added, *"Now, brothers, I know that you acted in ignorance, as did your leaders. But this is how God fulfilled what he had foretold through all the prophets, saying that his Christ would suffer. Repent, then, and turn to God, so that your sins may be wiped out, that times of refreshing [restoration] may come from the Lord, and that he may send the Christ, who has been appointed for you—even Jesus. He must remain in heaven until the time comes for God to restore everything, as he promised long ago through his holy prophets"* (Acts 3:17-21).

It is important to note that Christ is to remain in heaven (His place, Hosea 5:15) until the time comes to restore everything (the raising up, or restoration, spoken of in Hosea 6:2).

TIMES OF REFRESHING

We just saw above that the restoration is associated with the times of refreshing. The day of the Lord has long been associated by the Jews as a time of the kingdom, the time of restoration, and the time of refreshing. The Jews had a tendency to overlook the wrath of the day of the Lord, in spite of numerous warnings, such as this by Amos, the Prophet: *"Woe to you who long for the day of the Lord! Why do you long for the day of the Lord? That day will be darkness, not light"* (Amos 5:18).

What they longed for was the good news that the day of the Lord would bring. The good news of their refreshing in their restored kingdom will last for a thousand years (Rev. 20:1-7).

A DAY IS 1,000 YEARS

The Day of the Lord is to be 1,000 years in duration— a millennium (see Rev. 20:2, 3). *"...for [in] six days the Lord made heaven and earth, and on the seventh day he rested, and was refreshed"* (Exodus 31:17) (KJV). This millennium in the Old Testament is described as a "Sabbath keeping" period of rest, and is referred to as such in Hebrews 4:4-11, where it is associated with the seventh day of the creative week—a time to rest and be refreshed.

We now see that this seventh day corresponds to the seventh day of the week, and that it is 1,000 years in length. Therefore, it is not unwarranted to associate the other six days of God's creative week with the 6,000 years of man's "week," which continues to elapse.

In Hosea 6:2, "two days" and "on the third day" are mentioned. These "days" can only be on the scale of 1,000 years to a day. Scripture contains different time scales. A day can be a year (seven days (one week) represents seven years) as in the 70th week of Daniel (a period of seven years) (See also Ezek. 4:6.). A day can also be 1,000 years, as in Psalm 90:4, *"For a thousand years in your sight are like a day that has just gone by,"* and 2 Peter 3:8, *"With the Lord a day is like a thousand years, and a thousand years are like a day."*

Thus, we see that God can use a day to symbolize different units of time. The above days (in Hosea 6:2) cannot be literal days or even years, for many literal days and years have passed since Hosea's time. Hosea himself said this would be the case: *"For the Israelites will live many days without king or prince..."* (Hos. 3:4-5).

So Hosea's "days" are not 24-hour days, or one year days, but 1,000-year days.

RESTORATION ON THE THIRD DAY

It is both interesting and significant that while He was on the earth, Christ was rejected from Jerusalem for two days, and was raised on the third day. The Lord God is making Christ's brethren—Israel—a "type" of Himself, and is thoroughly keeping the law for them: *"An eye for an eye, and a tooth for a tooth."* As they rejected Christ, so God is rejecting the Israelites for two days, and will restore them on the third day. Let us take another look at Hosea 6:2: *"After two days he will revive us; on the third day he will restore us, that we may live in his presence."* Just as Israel's Christ was raised on the third day, Israel itself will be raised on the third day.

The late, great J. Vernon McGee also saw this parallel. In "Thru The Bible,"[13] he expounds on Hosea's prophetic passage: "'In the third day he will raise us up'—this is very

---

[13] Vol. 3, pp. 635-636, used with permission.

interesting in light of the fact that the resurrection of Christ was on the third day. He was raised for the justification of both Jew and Gentile. This will also be applicable in that future day when God will bring Israel back into that land and bring them to himself. In Ezekiel 37 God speaks of that day as a resurrection, and that resurrection will be based on the One who was raised on the third day; for in Christ's resurrection there is provided, for any man who will accept it, a redemption and a justification which will bring him into a right relationship with Almighty God.

"The apostle Paul develops the subject of the future of Israel in Romans 11. In our day, God's purpose in building his church is to draw to himself both Jew and Gentile, people out of every tongue and tribe and nation, who are going to come before him to worship. When God completes his purpose in the church and takes it out of the world, he will again turn to the nation Israel and will raise her up. Every prophet who wrote in Scripture—and even some who didn't write—spoke of God's future purpose for the nation Israel. Even before the children of Israel could get into the land, Moses began to talk about the coming day when God would restore them back to the land for the third time. The third time—on the third day, so to speak—the restoration to the land would be a permanent restoration. There is a correlation between this restoration and Christ's being raised from the dead on the third day."

THE MYSTERY
Overview of the Mystery

This author agrees with Dr. McGee's above perspective. However, this book is about the end of the age, about which Scripture prophesies. It is not about the Church Age, which exists at the time of this writing. In Dr. McGee's passage, he spoke of God taking out the present day Church, which is a mystery.[14] As discussed earlier, a mystery and a prophecy are far from the same thing! Prophecy can have a sign and a time (date), while a mystery is signless and timeless.

Let us diverge from prophecy momentarily to further examine the mystery, then return to "Restoration on the third day."

This Age ends, as has been shown, with the second coming of Jesus Christ in Rev. 1:7, *"Every eye shall see him."* The physical removal from the earth of the present day Mystery Church is what is popularly known as the Rapture. God will do this before He deals with an unrepentant Israel (and remaining prophecy), and certainly before the Antichrist or lawless one is revealed (2 Thess. 2:8).

The Mystery Church, with its Rapture, should really be the subject of another book, but since that will mark the end of the earthly pilgrimage for all believers as of the time of this writing, it might interest some to read of educated guesses as to the approximate time the Rapture will occur.[15]

When will the Rapture occur? One can only guess, for this is truly a mystery, as was affirmed by the Apostle Paul (1 Cor. 15:51), and is not a subject of Old Testament prophecy (Rom. 16:25; Col. 1:26).

Definition of the Mystery

The mystery is this: The body of believers in Christ, which have lived since the time of Christ and until the time of the Rapture, is a body in which Gentiles are able to

---

[14] See "Definition of the Mystery."

[15] It is possible, depending on when this book is read, that the Rapture may already have occurred. If so, there may be other opportunities to escape God's coming, escalating wrath (see "Feast of First Fruits" and "Feast of Rosh HaShanah" in this chapter).

come to God directly through Christ, the Jewish Messiah (Eph. 3:6)—without the birthright of God's chosen people, the Jews, or through adoption of Jewish Mosaic Law.[16]

Salvation was extended to the Gentiles because the Jews were not in a right relationship with God. They could have been a blessing to the rest of the world, yet to this day they continue to chafe under God's rejection.[17]

In a sense, the problem of an unrepentant Jewish nation has temporarily been set aside, while God carries on with business (Rom. 11:11-25). They're "on break," and are being disciplined. In the meantime, we who are believers by faith, having been sprinkled with the blood of Christ, are able to pass from the outer court of the temple directly into the Holy of Holies! We who are in Christ may go directly to the throne of God, and no longer need a Priest to intercede and make sacrifice for our sins.

The Old Testament prophets never saw this long break because it was not revealed to them (Eph. 3:5); *"The mystery that has been kept hidden for ages and generations…"* (Col. 1:26). Paul addressed both the Mystery and the Rapture.

Rapture Within The Mystery

"Listen, I tell you a mystery: We will not all sleep, but we will all be changed in a flash, in the twinkling of an eye, at the last trumpet" (1 Cor. 15:51-52).

Let's start guessing when this will happen, right now! It will happen sometime between the present and the time when the Antichrist signs a seven-year peace treaty with Israel.

---

[16] Non-Jews who became Jews by following Mosaic Law are called proselytes.

[17] Jews who come to faith in Christ the same as Gentiles become part of the Mystery Church.

The Bible gives a promise that the lawless one (the Antichrist) will not be revealed until the One who is restraining lawlessness is taken out of the way (2 Thess. 2:7-8). The One who is the restrainer could be none other than the Holy Spirit, indwelling and working through the body of believers, the Church.

The Bible also promises that God will never leave the believers (Heb. 13:5). Therefore, when the Holy Spirit is taken out of the way, the believers go with Him. We are told that this will be done before the Antichrist is positively identified or revealed (at least by the signing of the peace treaty with Israel). Since it will take time for the Antichrist to work his way into position for such an agreement, he will surely have revealed many indications of his identity before the actual signing ceremony. So, it is probable that the Church will be taken out of the way long before the ceremony, perhaps years earlier. The removal of the Church, and the Holy Spirit, will open the door for lawlessness to develop at an enhanced rate, thus opening the door for the lawless one to "solve" Israel's problems by signing a seven-year peace treaty at the beginning of the Jewish New Year (either on Rosh HaShanah or Yom Kippur).[18]

Letters to the Churches

If we examine closely the letters to the churches in Rev. 2-3, some very interesting things come to light. Many Bible expositors are correct, spiritually speaking, when they say those chapters give us the history of the Church from the time of Christ to the Rapture. But, more definitely, these chapters provide ongoing instruction throughout the tribulation. Many expositors say the Church isn't mentioned again after chapter 3, until we see

[18] Because the signing takes place seven years before the end, which as we will soon see, will occur at this time of the year.

it again in chapter 19. They therefore conclude that since the tribulation is between chapters 6-19, and since there is no instruction for the Church during that time, that the Church is raptured before the tribulation.

This author believes that instructions about what to do during the tribulation have already been provided in the book of Revelation, chapters two and three. These special chapters in Revelation offer many details to the Churches about how to proceed through the tribulation.

The solution to the enigma is that the Churches described in chapters two and three are believers who are receiving instructions during the time that evil is no longer being restrained. This body of believers is clearly very Jewish in nature, and is not the Mystery Church previously described. Rather, this is the body of believers who begin to profess Christ after the Mystery Church is raptured. The Rapture will be a monumental, worldwide event, and countless hearts will be immediately quickened as they realize—too late—that they should have believed sooner. Nevertheless, these new believers will comprise a new church—the Kingdom Church.

To reiterate: We know that iniquity or lawlessness (evil) is being restrained until someone is taken out. This could be none other than God, in the person of the Holy Spirit, working through His temple of believers. So the Holy Spirit, the Comforter—who will never leave us—leaves with us and evil is no longer restrained. After the Mystery Church is raptured, the Kingdom Church (the Tribulation Saints) faces terrible times. Indeed, it is called the Tribulation for good reason. It will be back to the way it was in the gospels— Matthew, Mark, Luke, and John. The gospel of the kindgom, rather than the gospel of grace, will be preached.

A Day Is A Year

We saw earlier that a scriptural day can be a physical year. From Jewish festival typology, we shall soon learn that Yom Kippur, the Jewish New Year, will be the chosen day of the Revelation of Jesus Christ.[19] There are 10 days between Rosh HaShanah and Yom Kippur. Rosh HaShanah is the blowing of the trumpets, and the ten days between them have been known as the Days of Awe. They are a time of testing, as were the 10 days of Daniel and the other princes' 10 days of testing.

We saw that a day is a year during the period of the week of Jacob's trouble. Thus, 10 days should be 10 years. If we could determine how long the next church (the Kingdom Church) was going to suffer under Satan—particularly when Satan's evil is no longer restrained—we would have a possible time for the Rapture of the Mystery Church, the coming of Jesus Christ to meet His saints in the clouds (1 Thess. 4:17).

The time of suffering is given: *"Fear none of those things which thou shalt suffer: behold, the devil shall cast [some] of you into prison, that ye may be tried; and ye shall have tribulation ten days: be thou faithful unto death, and I will give thee a crown of life"* (Rev. 2:10, KJV).

If we assume that great evil and suffering will break out when God no longer restrains evil; that God will begin to deal with the Kingdom Church right after the Rapture of the Mystery Church; that the 10 days in Rev. 2:10 are 10 years; then the Mystery Church (the present day Church) is taken to heaven (John 14:3) 10 years before the end. For example, if the end is at 2030 A.D.,

---

[19] See "Yom Kippur." All significant Church events occurred on Jewish holidays, i.e., crucifixion on Passover, resurrection on Feast of First Fruits, and the Holy Spirit on Pentecost. This significant event will as well.

that will make 2020 A.D. the time of the Rapture for the present day Mystery Church.

Type for the Mystery Church

Here are more educated guesses for you. God raised up other first fruits with Christ when He arose, and we (the born again believers) are all part of this first resurrection in Christ (1 Cor. 15:20, 23). If God uses the typology here, the dead in Christ (1 Thess. 4:16) may rise on the same calendar day that Christ arose. That day would be on the Sunday after the Spring full moon in Israel, which occurs on Nisan 14[20] (traditionally, after the almond blossoms bloom in Spring). That will then give those in the present day Mystery Church, who are alive and remain, 40 days (previous typology had this time element) before ascending or being raptured on the same day that Christ ascended. Hallelujah!

Let's now return to the discussion of prophecy and the resurrection/restoration on the third day.

RESTORATION ON THE THIRD DAY—Continued

Since we have established that the days of Hosea 6:2 are days of one thousand years each (as is the Millennial Day), we can now make calculations concerning the time when the end will come. Let's assume the time when God left (Christ was cut off) was 30 A.D.[21] If you add 30 A.D. + 2,000 years, you get 2030 A.D. This would be the beginning of the third day or the third 1,000 years!

---

[20] The first month of the sacred year, called Abib in the Pentateuch, for which it is substituted only in the time of the captivity (Neh. 2:1; Esth. 3:7).

[21] See "The Year of Messiah's Coming."

THE COUNT DOWN—GOD USES 490's

This date is also consistent with God's number of 490, or 70 sevens, from the book of Daniel. By overviewing history, it appears that God's dealings with the Hebrew race will involve four 70-week periods, each totaling 490 years (details to follow). However, the actual time of each period is not recorded to be precisely 490 years, something that can be determined by comparing scriptures. For example, during the second 70-week period, from the Exodus to the building of Solomon's temple, is shown in Acts 13:18-22 to total 591 years. I Kings 6:1 shows the same period of history to last 480 years. This discrepancy of 111 years is the total of six different periods during which Israel was in servitude to others (see the book of Judges)—when they were out of God's favor or will. Since we know that the Bible cannot contradict itself, what we should gather is that God does not include those years when Israel is out of favor.

Following is an explanation of the four 70 week periods:

(1) The first 70 weeks, or 490 years, was from the birth of Abraham to the Exodus. The actual time was 505 years but God didn't count the 15 years that Ishmael was a usurper.

(2) The second 70 weeks, or 490 years, was from the Exodus to the dedication (not the building) of Solomon's Temple. The actual time was 601 years, but God didn't include 111 years of servitude when Israel was out of favor.

(3) The third 70 weeks, or 490 years, was from the dedication of Solomon's Temple to the Edict of Artaxerxes. The actual time was 560 years, but God didn't count the 70 years of Babylonian captivity.

(4) The fourth 70 weeks, or 490 years, is from the Edict of Artaxerxes to the second coming of Christ. A total of 483 years elapsed from the Edict to the point that Messiah was cut off (Dan 9:25), and God has not included the period of time from then until the present. Therefore, there are still seven more years left to count, (the week of Jacob's trouble) before the completion of another 490-year period.

We see a pattern here! God clearly uses periods of time that are 490 years in duration, and it appears He will have used four 490's by the time Christ returns at the Revelation. We also see that God has not counted time for the Hebrews when they have been out of favor. Let us examine more closely this state of disfavor in the fourth 490 years.

The Temple was destroyed, and the Jews were dispersed in 70 A.D., marking God's disfavor with the Jewish nation. Are they still out of favor? As mentioned previously, we can assume that the Father answered the Son's prayer on the Cross: *"Father, forgive them for they do not know what they are doing"* (Luke 23:34), and that the Father did so by giving the Jews a 40-year testing, probationary period, after Christ's death.

It was then that the Jews were dispersed and are now out of favor. At present the nation is rebuilding, but this could not be the restoration on the third day because it doesn't fit prophecy. The true restoration will be done by God after the Revelation of Jesus Christ. If, as the scriptures seem to indicate, the year 2030 is the end, then an interesting note is created. There will have been four 490's, i.e. 4 x 490, or 1960 years from the time of their dispersion until the time of their restoration, i.e. when we add 1,960 to 70, it brings us to 2030 A.D.

Is God counting an equal amount of time against Israel

(the time they were out of His favor) as He has for Israel (the time they were in His favor)? If so, each would have a total of four time periods, i.e., 4 x 490 or 1,960 years.

These conclusions interpret the Hebrew passage, Hosea 6:2, to mean that after two days, and in the 3rd day, God would start the tribulation—at 2030 A.D. (after two days). The end then would be 2037 A.D.! This would indicate that God will again start His time clock (the one that stopped after 483 years) and let the countdown begin for the last seven years of man's "rule."

This may make more sense. Each clock, the one for and the one against Israel, will have ticked off the same number of years. Thus, since the dispersion, God will have counted (on separate clocks) an equal amount of time when the Jews were out of favor as when they were not in captivity or servitude.

The Year of Messiah's Coming

To determine when the end is, we need to know when the decree to restore and rebuild Jerusalem of Daniel 9:25 was issued, when the Messiah came to His people, and the length of the gap of time. We see that the gap will be for 2 days (Hos. 6:2), so we will add that to when He came. We now need the exact year the Messiah came.

In Nehemiah 2:1-8, the 69 weeks began in the month of Nisan, in the 20th year of King Artaxerxes. He began his reign in 465 B.C., and issued his decree on March 14, 445 B.C. God's prophetic years are 360 days in length.[22] Using the scale of a day is a year, then 69 weeks x 7 (days/week) = 483 days, or 483 years. Thus, 483 years x 360 days/year

---

[22] From Gen. 7:11-24; 8:3-4, we learn that 5 months from the 17th day of the second month to the 17th day of the seventh month is 150 days, or 30 days to the month. See " A Day Is A Year," this chapter.

= 173,880 days. In today's calendars, 173,880 days converted to 365 1/4 days/year = 476.06 years. That is 476 years and 22 days added to 445 B.C. brings us to 31 A.D. We subtract 1 year when we cross from B.C. to A.D. This brings us into the first week of April, 30 A.D., which is the appointed day for Messiah to ride into Jerusalem.

It is during this week that Jesus said, *"If you, even you, had only known on this day what would bring you peace—but now it is hidden from your eyes. The days will come upon you when your enemies will build an embankment against you and encircle you and hem you in on every side. They will dash you to the ground, you and the children within your walls. They will not leave one stone on another, because you did not recognize the time of God's coming to you"* (Luke 19:42-44).

From history, we know that the above days, of which Christ spoke, were fulfilled when Titus destroyed the temple in 70 A.D. We see in this passage that the 70 A.D. event had been prophesied, and now understand that the prophecy was spoken in 30 A.D. This passage shows a relationship between 30 A.D. and 70 A.D., when prophecy was fulfilled only 40 years after it was spoken— a quick fulfillment of Biblical prophecy. When Messiah was asked by His disciples in Matthew 24, *"...when will this happen..."* (the stones not being left upon another), the Lord gave them several prophecies.

The destruction of the temple was the prophecy that was only 40 years away. He also spoke of several end time events. God gave us one prophecy that happened quickly. This way, we of so little faith can believe that the distant prophecies will occur as well. The reality is that virtually all of the different end time events revealed in scripture have been shown to be separated by great periods of time. This current period of time in which we live will be 2 days in length, or 2,000 years. If we add 30 A.D. to 2000 we get 2030 A.D. This is either the year the tribulation starts (with the signing of a peace treaty by the false messiah) or the year of the Revelation of Jesus Christ when the false messiah comes to his end.

We now see that the two days (or 2,000 years) are to be added to the time when Christ ascended (30 A.D., after He had been "cut off") and not when He came to earth, via His birth (4 B.C.); which is something that many Bible teachers and students believe in error, as of the time of this writing.

The Last 490

In Dan. 9:25, the Bible prophesied 483 years to the Messiah: *"From the issuing of the decree to restore and rebuild Jerusalem until the Anointed One, the ruler, comes, there will be seven 'sevens,' and sixty-two 'sevens.'"* The Messiah came in His "triumphal" entry (riding a donkey) on Nisan 10, 30 A.D. This is the day the Jews were to inspect the lamb (Exod. 12:3, 5). This fulfilled Zech. 9:9—*"See, your king comes to you, righteous and having salvation, gentle and riding on a donkey."* The next verse (Zech. 9:10) picks up after our gap of 2,000 years ((4 x 490) + 40 years of probation + 30 A.D.). It speaks of taking away implements of war and of ruling during a time of peace. This is where Romans 11:26 will be fulfilled in that *"...all Israel will be saved."* That is, all who are left after the Tribulation (and the Antichrist) come to an end. Only then can peace begin.

Since the inspection of the lamb for the sacrifice and the sacrifice of the lamb are only four days apart (respectively, Nisan 10 and Nisan 14); then the "triumphal" entry of the Sacrificial Lamb and the crucifixion were to be only four days apart. This fulfills the double prophecy of Dan. 9:25-26—"until he comes" and His being "cut off"—as both taking place during the same week, and two days before the weekly Sabbath. (The crucifixion was the day before a High Sabbath—see the section, "Feast of Unleavened Bread" in this chapter.)

Earlier, we saw that Israel is a type of the Messiah. It seems then, that the two days of Hosea 6:2 coincide with the two days between the crucifixion and the weekly Sabbath, or the gap of time in which we presently live; where Israel has been set aside, but is soon to be revived, a period of time which will be 2,000 years in length (two days). Then, the weekly Sabbath will be typical of the peace on the third day, a 1,000 year Sabbath. At this time, the inscription at the United Nations building in New York will be fulfilled: "*...and they shall beat their swords into plowshares, and their spears into pruninghooks: nation shall not lift up sword against nation, neither shall they learn war any more*" (Isa. 2:4).

Through scripture, it appears that God has given us the year of the Revelation of Jesus Christ. Have we been given the day?

Typical Prophecy Sets Dates

Dates (days) are set by God in what is known as typical prophecy. The seven annual Jewish festivals are all date setting and "typical prophetic" events! The riddle is to figure out what the festival is about and then one has the exact day on which the "festival typical" event will occur. Since nearly four of the festivals have been fulfilled, we can easily verify this reality, as we will see below.

These festivals are known as convocations, which literally mean rehearsals. This is a time when God explains, defines, demonstrates, reinforces, and sets dates about His master plan of redemption and restoration through the Messiah—for two distinctly different earthly appearances.

THE SPRING FESTIVALS
Feast Of Passover

Passover, the first festival or feast, is celebrated on Nisan 14. It commemorates the time the Israelites were slaves in Egypt, when God raised up a deliverer—Moses. Moses wanted Pharaoh to let God's people go for a three-day journey into the desert, there to offer sacrifices to God (Exod. 3:18). After nine plagues, the unconvinced Pharaoh needed one more! It was then, on the 10th day of Nisan, that God instructed them to take a lamb without spot or blemish, and to inspect it for four days. On the 14th day they were to slay the lamb "in the evening" (Exod 12:6). This should be translated in the Bible as "between the two evenings." This would place the slaying of the Passover Lamb between the minor and major evening oblations, which ran from 12:00 noon to 6:00 p.m., or at 3:00 p.m., which was the ninth hour (the ninth hour of sunlight). This is the same time of day during the Festival of Passover that Christ died on the cross (Matt. 27:45-46).

Feast Of Unleavened Bread

Three hours later, at 6:00 p.m., the next Jewish day begins. This is the Feast of Unleavened Bread, and as such, it becomes a sabbath day, regardless of the day of the week on which it occurs. Such days are known as high sabbaths—the first of seven high sabbaths in the Jewish year.[23]

On this day, the 15th day of Nisan, the Jews prepare

---

[23] Due to the lack of this knowledge, and the fact that Christ was crucified before a sabbath, most Christians celebrate an erroneous Good Friday. Non-Jewish tradition has created a physical impossibility, with three days and three nights of Christ's state of death (Matt. 12:40) occurring between Friday night and Sunday morning.

unleavened bread, which symbolizes holiness. The preparations include wrapping and "securing" a piece of bread.

―――――――――――――― ⟲⟲⟲ ――――――――――――――

This piece of unleavened bread that is "wrapped" during the Passover meal—afikomen, a Greek term—literally means "the one who came."

―――――――――――――― ⟲⟲⟲ ――――――――――――――

In ancient days, it had been on the 15th of Nisan that the Jews began their exodus from Egypt. Also Joseph, son of Jacob, had made a request that his bones be picked up, or "secured" at his grave when the Israelites returned to the promised land. It was on the 15th of Nisan, at the beginning of their exodus, that Joseph's request was granted. In a climactic moment of prophetic fulfillment and historical significance, this is the same day Christ's body was prepared and secured in the tomb of Joseph of Arimathea.

Feast Of First Fruits

The next festival is the Feast of First Fruits, celebrated on the first Sunday (the day after the weekly Sabbath) after Nisan 15. This commemorates the day that the Israelites crossed the dreadful Red Sea and came out alive on the other side, a "resurrected" people. Such an important day did not go unnoticed by Christ. He descended into hell, and rose up alive on this day—Christ was resurrected on the Feast of First Fruits.

This feast is also known as the Fruits of the Barley Harvest. It is at this time that the Messiah, and others who had been resurrected from the dead, were seen.[24] In the

―――――――――――――――――

[24] At the same time, many others also rose from the dead (Matthew 27:50, 52).

New Testament, it is spoken of as the first fruits of the resurrection of the dead (1 Cor. 15:20). Also, in prophecy yet remaining, Christ is depicted as the first fruits of all believers who will be resurrected; and when He comes again, those who belong to Him will rise again to be with Him (1 Cor. 15:23). There is every reason to believe it will occur on this very day!

We see in the Book of James that the Jews are addressed in this book, for they are the "twelve tribes scattered among the nations." James shows that the Jews who chose re-birth (became "born again" believers) through the Word of Truth are a firstfruits (James 1:18). Further, there appears to be a resurrection on the day of the Feast of First Fruits—in the middle of the tribulation. Michael the Archangel is God's warrior, for he is seen warring with Satan in heaven during the middle of the tribulation, and kicking him out (Rev. 12:6,7). Michael has also been associated with resurrection, for he is shown to be the one with whom Satan was disputing over the body of Moses (Jude 9).

The Old Testament saints are raised after the saints, who have believed in Christ (the Mystery Church) are raised. The Bible states, *"the dead in Christ will rise first"* (1 Thess. 4:16). This is because the Old Testament saints lived prior to the Day of Pentecost, before the Holy Spirit came and placed New Testament saints in Christ (1 Cor. 12:12-13; Acts 1:5).

Daniel the prophet gives us the time for the resurrection of the Old Testament Jews. *"At that time Michael, the great prince who protects your people, will arise. There will be a time of distress such as has not happened from the beginning of nations until then. But at that time your people, everyone whose name is found written in the book will be delivered. Multitudes who sleep in the dust of the earth will*

89

awake: some to everlasting life, others to shame and ever-lasting contempt" (Dan. 12:1-2).

Christ identified the time above as being at the time of *"...the abomination that causes desolation"* (Matt. 24:15), and that it would be the beginning of great tribulation. *"For then there will be great distress, unequaled from the beginning of the world until now and never to be equaled again"* (Matt. 24:21).

Michael throws Satan out of heaven with 1,260 days left in the tribulation (Rev 12:6). It appears then, that Michael is going to follow him, for Michael is present at the resurrection of the Old Testament Jews (as seen above), and will dispute with Satan once again!

In Daniel 12:1, nothing is mentioned about a transla-tion (a rapture) for those who are alive. But perhaps there is, for a male child is snatched up to God at that time (Rev. 12:5). This male child cannot be Christ as many believe, because He has already ascended. The male child has to be Jewish because his mother is Jewish—clothed with the sun. Jacob interpreted this symbolism as being Israel (Gen. 37:9-11).

This male *child "...will rule the nations with an iron scepter"* (Rev. 12:5). Since this is what is said about God's Son (Psalm 2:7-9), the Messiah—many believe it is Him, and Him alone. But, the Messiah (Christ) addresses the churches in the Book of Revelation, chapters 2 and 3, which are clearly Jewish. To the Church in Thyatira, He warns them of Jezebel, who led the Jews to Baal with her sexual immorality and eating food sacrificed to idols (Rev. 2:20). He tells those who are unwilling to repent, that they will suffer *"great tribulation"* (Rev. 2:22, KJV). However, He said those individuals who did not hold to Jezebel's teaching would not have that burden imposed on them (Rev. 2:24), and that they would have authority over the nations: *"He will rule them with an iron scepter; he will dash them to pieces like pottery"* (Rev. 2:27).

So, we see that the male child will include the believing, true Jews of the Church of Thyatira, and that they have received a promise of escaping the great tribulation (others also have been promised escape, in Rev. 3:10). Here we are shown that there is merit in believing that there may be a rapture during the middle of the tribulation. This makes a lot of sense, because these new Jewish believers will escape the greatest tribulation—the time when God's wrath is to become unbearable. Surely, other Christians (non-Jewish believers or Gentiles) will be raptured from all over the world as well. For there is no distinction between Jews and Gentiles in the Church, for they are *"...members together of one body, and sharers together in the promise in Christ Jesus"* (Eph. 3:6).

It makes good sense that there will be a rapture just before the great tribulation, which begins at the middle of the seven-years of Jacob's trouble. The Lord tells His Jewish brethren, the people who have found themselves in this seven-year time of trouble (Luke 21; Matt. 24), to be on the lookout for Him to come. He tells them two things that would at first appear to be a contradiction: He is to come like a thief in the night (Matt. 24:43-44; Luke 12:29-31)—yet also with very apparent signs announcing His coming (Matt. 24:29-31).

The apparent contradiction is solved if two different comings are described. Since the well announced coming is after the great distress, the tribulation (Matt. 24:29), then another coming before the end would solve the enigma. The Messiah warns those who are to see Jerusalem surrounded by armies (as it was in 70 A.D.), that its desolation is near (Luke 21:20). They are to flee, for it is the time of the prophesied punishment to be fulfilled. This occurs at the middle of the tribulation. He gives them instruction and admonition:

"Be always on the watch, and pray that you may be able to escape all that is about to happen, and that you may be able to stand before the Son of Man" (Luke 21:36).

It seems clear that this is ongoing evidence of another escape, a mid-tribulational rapture.

The "Lord's Prayer" is much needed by these believers, and indeed this group has need of this prayer: *"And lead us not into temptation [testing], but deliver us from the evil one [the Antichrist]"* (Matt. 6:13).

Note that the Bible refers to the great tribulation as a time of testing (Rev. 3:10).

Other Old Testament passages support a mid-tribulational rapture:

"The righteous [vanish],...*and merciful men [are] taken away, none considering that the righteous is taken away from the evil* [to come]" (Isa. 57:1, KJV).

Here is some speculation to consider: If the Jewish Kingdom Churches of Revelation (chapters 2 and 3) all exist at the same time; and the Church at Smyrna is to be raptured at the middle of the tribulation with the believers of the other Churches; and the 10 days of Smyrna's persecution is 10 years; and God begins to build these Kingdom Churches immediately after the rapture of the Mystery Church of today, then that would place the rapture of the Church (at the time of this writing) thirteen and a half years before the end.

Counting Of The Omer

The forty-nine days that connect the Feast of First Fruits to the Feast of Pentecost, are known as the Counting of the Omer. Anciently, Moses told Pharaoh to let God's people go. Pharaoh pursued the Israelites as they left Egypt, but the Lord miraculously delivered them by parting the Red Sea. They continued on into the wilderness, reaching Mt. Sinai forty-nine days later.

In the future, at the middle of the tribulation, it appears that Moses, who most likely is one of the two witnesses of Revelation 11:3, will lead the Jews once again—this time away from the Antichrist. The Antichrist will send an army after the Jews as they flee from Jerusalem, when the abomination of desolation is accomplished. As the Jews flee into the wilderness, they will be delivered on eagles' wings (Rev. 12:14). It will be on the same eagles' wings (Exod. 19:4) that the Jews were miraculously delivered from Pharaoh during the Exodus.

The two witnesses are probably Moses and Elijah. Perhaps Elijah will be acting as Aaron did 3,500 years earlier.

Revelation, chapter 12 is full of symbolism. The dragon is defined as Satan, the ancient serpent. From the mouth of the symbolic serpent comes a flood or river (which has to be symbolic as well). A flood is symbolic of armies (Jer. 46:8) which are to be swallowed by the earth (Rev. 12:16); analogous to the Egyptian armies of Pharaoh being swallowed by the water (Exod. 15:12). The Jews who flee are those who obey their Messiah's words: *"So when you see standing in the holy place 'the abomination that causes desolation,' spoken of through the prophet Daniel—let the reader understand—then let those who are in Judea flee to the mountains"* (Matt. 24:15-16).

It appears that one place to which they flee may be Petra, or Sela (Isa. 16:1-5).[25] As in the wilderness, Christ

---

[25] Petra has a long, narrow entrance as the only way in, typical of a sheep-fold or sheep pen.

will again provide them with manna, for there is no other way to sustain life in a desert. The fugitives will petition with the Lord's Prayer that Christ gave as an example: *"Give us today our daily bread* [Manna]..." (Matt. 6:11).

Feast Of Pentecost

The next feast is the Feast of Pentecost, which is fifty days after the Barley Harvest. Many believe that this feast has been completely fulfilled. If one examines this feast closely, he will see that it has only been partially fulfilled. Not all that was spoken of by Joel the Prophet was fulfilled at Pentecost, which occurred 10 days after Christ's ascension. What was seen anciently at the Revelation of God on Mt. Sinai (which was on the same day as Pentecost)—the fire, the wind, and tongues—were the same that were observed by those in attendance with Peter the Apostle on the Day of Pentecost (Acts 2:2-3).[26]

However, the blood, fire, and billows of smoke; and the sun and moon darkening (Joel 2:30-31; Acts 2:19; Rev 9:2-3) were not seen. This happens in the middle and at the end of the seven years of the Tribulation (The Week of Jacob's Trouble, yet in the future).[27]

Since today's Church is a mystery and not the subject of prophecy, and Pentecost is the prophesied Wheat Harvest, then there is yet a future harvest, not involving the Church of today.[28] So, the Pentecost which occurs

---

[26] Further, as the Law was inscribed on stone tablets through Moses, so the Holy Spirit came to inscribe God's laws on men's hearts through Peter.

[27] At these times, the sign seekers (the Jews) will see the signs they sought, and were promised by their prophet Joel.

[28] This is because the Church is not destined for punishment with unbelievers who are receiving God's wrath (1 Thess. 5:9).

near the middle of the seven-year tribulation will hold a harvest for some souls at that time. This leaves the second part of the fulfillment of Pentecost for the Jews.

The future Pentecost will be the Wheat Harvest for the Jews who will be going through the last half of the tribulation. There will be a remnant left from Israel who will have seen the miraculous events, engineered by the divine hand of Christ, and will be born anew. In the time of Moses, on the Day of Pentecost, the presence of God empowered His people for obedience with His laws. In the time of Christ, also on the Day of Pentecost, the Holy Spirit empowered His people with the fire of God's presence in their hearts. In the same way, the future Day of Pentecost will empower others with an anointing fire and wind of God's holy presence. A total of 144,000 witnesses will have been sealed (Rev. 7:4), and these strategic witnesses will carry out, in God's power, Christ's great commission to teach all nations (Matt. 28:19). When the gospel of the Kingdom is preached as *"a testimony to all nations...then the end will come"* (Matt. 24:14).

THE FALL FESTIVALS

The remaining three feasts are celebrated in the fall. As observed above, the details of the earlier festival's events were fulfilled in every way at the proper time; so will be the fulfillment of those remaining. Again, by understanding with what history and prophecy each feast is associated, we will be able to determine the day in which God's plan of restoring man and the earth through the Messiah will occur. Just as the other feasts have been literally and chronologically fulfilled, so will those that remain. The pattern is easy to follow, and with only a little faith we can believe the same pattern will continue.

Feast Of Rosh Hashanah

The fifth feast is Rosh HaShanah, or the Blowing of the Trumpets. It falls on the first day of the seventh religious month (the first month of the civil or agricultural year).

Joseph Good, in his book, "Rosh HaShanah and the Messianic Kingdom to Come,"[29] defines the many parallels associated with Rosh HaShanah: "Yom Teruah, the feast of Trumpets, is also called Rosh HaShanah (literally 'Head of the Year'), the Jewish New Year. It teaches about the coronation and wedding of the Messiah, the rewards of the court, the oseif (gathering of the nobles), the Day of Judgement, beginning of the Messianic kingdom, Jacob's Trouble, the resurrection of the dead, Teshuvah, and the birthday of the world (p. 43).

"The shofar[30] was used to announce the beginning of festivals, to muster troops, to warn of danger, to assemble the people, in the midst of battles, and for coronations (p. 81)."

We have to be careful when searching the Bible for references on the sounding of trumpets. This is because the trumpet sounds not only on Rosh HaShanah but at other feasts and events as well: *"Sound the ram's horn at the New Moon, and when the moon is full, on the day of our feast"* (Psalm 81:3).

But the Lord has spoken specifically about the feast of trumpets to Moses, *"Say to the Israelites: 'On the first day of the seventh month you are to have a day of rest, a sacred assembly commemorated with trumpet blasts. Do no regular work, but present an offering made to the Lord by fire'"* (Lev. 23:24-25).

---

[29] Hatikva Ministries, Port Arthur, Texas, p. 43, 81; used with permission.

[30] A ram's horn, which is blown as a trumpet.

Let's examine passages that support these different events of Rosh HaShanah, and discover what will happen on that same very significant day in the future.

Mustering of Troops

As stated above, the trumpet sounds for the mustering of troops. In the 4th and 51st chapters of Jeremiah, the day of the Lord is in view. There are proclamations to Jerusalem about a besieging army advancing against her:

"Oh, my anguish, my anguish! I writhe in pain. Oh, the agony of my heart! My heart pounds within me, I cannot keep silent. For I have heard the sound of the trumpet; I have heard the battle cry. Disaster follows disaster; the whole land lies in ruins. In an instant my tents are destroyed, my shelter in a moment. How long must I see the battle standard and hear the sound of the trumpet" (Jer. 4:19-21)?

"Lift up a banner in the land! Blow the trumpet among the nations! Prepare the nations for battle against her" (Jer. 51:27).

These passages show that there are to be trumpets as armies of the Antichrist head for Jerusalem just before the day of the Lord. The whole chapter of Ezekiel 7 is dedicated to this horrific end time event. It describes the coming battle of Armageddon, at the time of the Revelation. Since nations will come from everywhere to battle in Israel, the odds will overwhelm Israel with fear and helplessness.

"Son of man, this is what the Sovereign Lord says to the land of Israel: The end! The end has come upon the four corners of the land. The end is now upon you and I will unleash my anger against you. An unheard of disaster is coming. The end has come! The end has come!... The time has come, the day has arrived. Though they blow the trumpet and get

everything ready, no one will go into battle, for my wrath is against the whole crowd" (Ezek. 7:2-3, 5-6, 12, 14).

Apparently, trumpets were sounded for 30 days prior to Rosh HaShanah. This would be during the month of Elul, during the season of Teshuvah (the time of repentance). The last trumpet was heard on the day of Rosh HaShanah. In the future, with this last trumpet, the Day of the Lord is officially announced as coming in 10 days! The 10 "Days of Awe" officially begin at Rosh HaShanah— 10 days before the Revelation of Jesus the Messiah as Jehovah God Almighty on Yom Kippur! It appears that the 10 days of awe end with a great trumpet on that day of the Lord. In Zephaniah, chapter 1, the Day of the Lord is defined as a day of trumpet and battle cry.

"That day will be a day of wrath, a day of distress and anguish, a day of trouble and ruin, a day of darkness and gloom, a day of clouds and blackness, a day of trumpet and battle cry against the fortified cities and against the corner towers. Their blood will be poured out like dust and their entrails like filth. In the fire of His jealousy, the whole world will be consumed, for He will make a sudden end of all who live in the earth" (Zeph. 1:15-18).

Examination, Rapture, & Resurrection

Elul, the thirty-day month before Rosh HaShanah is the beginning of a 40-day period known as Teshuvah. In this Jewish period, a man is to examine his relationship with God because Rosh HaShanah, "The Day of Judgement," is approaching. Penitential prayers begin about one week before Rosh Hashanah, when individuals are to search their hearts and return to God. They believe that three groups of people will be judged at that time. One group is placed in the Book of the Righteous, one group is placed in the Book of the Wicked, while the destiny of the third group is not sealed for another 10 days. At Yom Kippur, the third group's final fate is sealed in one book or the other.[31]

For those who receive or have received the Lord, they may be able to escape His coming wrath by being raptured on Rosh HaShanah, perhaps 10 days before the end: *"...before the appointed time arrives...before the day of the Lord's wrath comes upon you. Seek the Lord, all you humble of the land, you who do what he commands. Seek righteousness, seek humility; perhaps you will be sheltered on the day of the Lord's anger"* (Zeph. 2:2-3).

Many have stated that there cannot be a rapture at the end of the tribulation. This is because there would be no saved people left on the earth to enter the Millennium. They understand that the judgement of the "sheep and goats" (Matt. 25:32-33) is prerequisite to entering the Millennium. But they don't understand that this judgement is based on works and not salvation! There is only mention of works here, and one is not saved by works (Rom. 3:21-26). Thus salvation,[32] not being a criteria for entering the Millennium, allows the unsaved to enter.

Earlier, we saw what appears to be a mid-tribulational rapture, which should occur in connection with the mid-tribulational resurrection (Dan. 12:1-2). The verses below appear to be for those who were not believers at the mid-tribulational rapture. *"The godly have been swept from the land; not one upright man remains. The day of your watchmen has come, the day God visits you. But as for me, I watch in*

---

[31] "Celebration, The Book of Jewish Festivals," Yossi Prager, Jonathan David Publishers, Inc., Middle Village, NY, p. 15.

[32] Salvation is defined as being placed/baptized (identified with) into the body of Christ, by the Holy Spirit (1 Cor. 12:13; Gal. 3:27).

hope for the Lord, I wait for God my Savior; my God will hear me. He will bring me out into the light" (Micah 7:2, 4, 7, 9).

This coming into the light is also associated with resurrection. *"Wake up, O sleeper, rise from the dead, and Christ will shine on you"* (Eph. 5:14).

"Seek the Lord, all you humble of the land, you who do what he commands. Seek righteousness, seek humility; perhaps you will be sheltered on the day of the Lord's anger" (Zeph. 2:3).

In John 11:24-25, Martha, like most other Jews, was aware of a resurrection at the last day. Jesus showed that one does not have to wait until the last day when He ordered Lazarus to rise from the grave. In doing so, He gave the Jews proof of who would do the resurrecting. He also gave the criteria for it when He said, *"I am the resurrection, and the life. He who believes in me will live, even though he dies; and whoever lives and believes in me will never die"* (John 11:25, 26).

In the above verses, Christ speaks of the last day. Those in Christ who have died before the last day will be resurrected then. Those who believe and are alive at the end will never die. It appears that those living believers at the end will be raptured. In other instances, there was a rapture at the time of a resurrection, thus paving the way for this end time resurrection to also be accompanied by a rapture. There will be those who come to faith in Jesus the Messiah as their Savior who live between the previous resurrection and rapture (at the middle of the tribulation) and Rosh Hashanah (at the end), who will be waiting expectantly on God. A final rapture 10 days before the end will enable the last of those who attain faith in Christ to be quickly judged by fire, and escape the greatest of wrath—the seven bowls of wrath and the Day of the Lord!

In Jewish literature, Rosh HaShanah is known as the

last trumpet. This is the last trumpet blown during Teshuvah (the 40-day season of repentance), and at the time which begins the 10 High Holy Days—the Days of Awe.

In 1 Thess. 4:17, the apostle Paul speaks of a resurrection and a changing (in preparation for a rapture or translation) at the last trump for some future believers (1 Cor. 15:51-52). This will fulfill the prophecies in the Old Testament, in which the prophets placed their hope (Hos. 13:14; Isa. 25:8). The type for this calling out and meeting God is found in the Old Testament. The scriptures show that at the blowing of trumpets, God's people were to set out and to meet at the Tent of Meeting. The Tent of Meeting is the tabernacle (Num. 9:15). This was a copy and shadow of what is in heaven (Heb. 8:5). In the past, the Lord has appeared to the entire assembly in front of the Tent of Meeting (Lev. 9:5). *"Make two trumpets of hammered silver, and use them for calling the community together and for having the camps set out. When both are sounded, the whole community is to assemble before you at the entrance to the Tent of Meeting"* (Num. 10:2-3).

Silver is the metal that symbolizes redemption. The above trumpets were made of the atonement money of the people. The first trumpet was used for the calling of the assembly and the last trumpet was used for the journeying of the camps. Later in Numbers, the Israelites were told that when an enemy was oppressing them, they were to sound the trumpets, and that the Lord would remember them and rescue them from their enemies (Num. 10:9). They were told specifically to do this at the feasts and New moon festivals (Num. 10:10).

According to the above passages in Numbers, the assembly is gathered and moved by the blowing of the trumpets. Thus, those that have received the Messiah will be gathered and moved to the gate of the assembly (the heavenly tabernacle) by the blowing of trumpets. Since the "clouds" or the New Jerusalem comes to the earth, a group of believers are to meet the Lord outside His heavenly tabernacle, which comes to the earth with the blowing of the last trumpet. They are in effect hidden from God's wrath, fulfilling the following: *"For in the day of trouble he will keep me safe in his dwelling; he will hide me in the shelter of his tabernacle and set me high upon a rock"* (Psalm 27:5).

Rosh HaShanah is the only festival that falls at the time of a new moon (when the moon is hidden or concealed), which explains why it is also known as The Day of Concealment. Believers will thus be concealed or hidden from the next 10 days, known as the High Holy Days, and as Tamin Nora'im (The Days of Awe).

Not only do those who come to believe in the Messiah escape the coming 10 Days of Awe, they are present for the coronation and wedding of the Messiah!

Coronation of the King

Trumpets sound at the crowning of a King! With his continual fighting of enemies, King David was a type of Tribulational Messiah. With his reign of glory and peace, King Solomon was a type of Millennial Messiah. Instruction was given to anoint Solomon as king over Israel and to do so with a trumpet blast (1 Kings 1:34). The Rosh HaShanah judgement and the gathering of believers to the shelter of God's tabernacle is accompanied with the coronation of the King and the blasting of trumpets.

"God has ascended amid shouts of joy, the Lord amid the sounding of trumpets. Sing praises to God, sing praises; sing praises to our King, sing praises. For God is the King of all the earth" (Psalm 47:5-7).

The last trumpet of Rosh Hashanah may also coincide

with the last trumpet in the book of Revelation. When the seventh angel sounds his trumpet (the last trumpet of the seventh seal in the book of Revelation), there will be loud voices in heaven saying: *"The kingdom of the world has become the kingdom of our Lord and of his Christ, and he will reign for ever and ever"* (Rev. 11:15).

This coronation coincides with the One (Jesus Christ) given authority, as prophesied in the book of Daniel.

"He approached the Ancient of Days and was led into his presence. He was given authority, glory and sovereign power; all peoples, nations and men of every language worshiped him. His dominion is an everlasting dominion that will not pass away, and his kingdom is one that will never be destroyed" (Dan. 7:13-14).

Judgement

Along with this coronation at Rosh HaShanah, one can see the concurrent judgement by this new King, better known as God Almighty, the one who is (I am that I am— Jehovah—the one who is alive), and the one who was (the one who was dead—Messiah Ben Joseph; Rev. 1:18).

This judgement is for Israel and the nations against Israel—after the Antichrist is destroyed and apparently just after Rosh Hashanah. This will be frightening, for it will surely involve death for some, the first death. Imagine how frightened those who do not have Christ will be at the white throne judgement 1,000 years later. At that judgement—the second death—everyone who does not belong to Christ is thrown into the Lake of Fire (Rev. 20:14) after their appearance before Him, Who said not to fear the first death, but the second one (Matt. 10:28).

"We give thanks to you, Lord God Almighty, the One who is and who was, because you have taken your great power and have begun to reign. The nations were angry; and your wrath has come. The time has come for judging the dead, and for rewarding your servants the prophets and your saints and those who reverence your name, both small and great; and for destroying those who destroy the earth" (Rev. 11:17-18).

Wedding of Messiah

Let's return to the good news, the Wedding at Rosh Hashanah. Everybody enjoys a wedding; Christ Himself attended a wedding in Cana. At that wedding, He created wine to assure the unbroken enjoyment of the guests.[33]At His own wedding feast, we can be assured that our enjoyment will be unbroken. As King Jesus begins His eternal reign, the royal wedding of weddings will commence!

"Then I heard what sounded like a great multitude, like the roar of rushing waters and like loud peals of thunder, shouting: 'Hallelujah! For our Lord God Almighty reigns. Let us rejoice and be glad and give him glory! For the wedding of the Lamb has come, and his bride has made herself ready'" (Rev. 19:6-7).

The actual banquet supper (after the wedding) is spoken of in verse 9, and takes place on the mountain in Israel (Isa. 25:6).[34]

We could rightly expect no less than the richest of symbolism for the marriage of Christ and His bride, the Church. In Jewish wedding tradition, a betrothal was

---

[33] This wedding took place on the third day (John 2:1).

[34] Apparently, right after the great supper of God, where the Antichrist is destroyed and the flesh of the people in his ranks are eaten by the buzzards (Rev. 19:17-18).

arranged by the father of the young man, by an agent, or by the young man himself. The bride was bought with a price. She spent a period of time waiting for the wedding, while the bride groom went to his father's house to prepare a place for her.

The groom had two friends, aptly known as "the friends of the bridegroom." They functioned as the two witnesses required for a Jewish wedding. One assisted the bride, the other was stationed with the bridegroom, and together they witnessed the marriage contract and ceremony. The couple spent seven days at a special chamber called a chupah. Here the groom gave gifts to the bride. Outside, the wedding guests waited for the friend of the bridegroom to announce that the marriage was consummated. At the announcement, great rejoicing broke out in a week-long celebration.

In the above traditional Jewish wedding, we can see many types: the father is God the Father, and the agent is God the Holy Spirit.[35] At the Passover meal, Jesus spoke as a bridegroom: *"In my father's house are many rooms; if it were not so, I would have told you. I am going there to prepare a place for you. And if I go and prepare a place for you, I will come back and take you to be with me that you also may be where I am"* John 14:3).

It is Jesus, in the parable of Matthew 13:44-45, who sold everything He had, and bought a pearl of great price (the bride). 1 Cor 6:20; 7:23 remind the bride that she is "bought at a price." John the Baptist is a type of friend of the bridegroom, who makes this declaration himself (John 3:29). The other friend of the bridegroom, the one assigned to the bride, is seen in Moses, who leads Israel.

---

[35] Symbolized by Eliezer, the one commissioned by Abraham, the father of Issac, to get a bride for his son; a type of God the Son.

With this background, we can understand when and why the two witnesses arise from the dead at Revelation 11, and perhaps who they are. In that chapter, the Lord is speaking of the Jewish Temple. The two witnesses are concerned with the Jews in the inner court, rather than the outer court of the Gentiles. They are seen as olive trees and lampstands, which are typical Jewish symbols. They strike the earth so there is no rain for 3 1/2 years, and inflict other plagues. Since there is no damage to the earth up until the time between the sixth seal and the first trumpet (Rev. 7:3), these Jewish witnesses are prophetical in the last half of the seven-year tribulation.

When they are through with their work, the Antichrist slays them. They will lie for 3 1/2 days in a street of Jerusalem, a day for each year of their prophecy (Rev. 11:3, 11). They are refused burial, so those of the world rejoice over them and view their dead bodies. However, the celebration is interrupted when they rise from the dead![36] Their resurrection is for a very special purpose: They will be the two witnesses for the Lamb's wedding (which will occur on/or near Tishri 1,[37] or Rosh HaShanah). So it appears that they will rise at that time (Rev. 11:11-15).

It has long been speculated that these two witnesses are either Elijah and Enoch, or Elijah and Moses. Since Enoch was not Jewish, this leaves Elijah and Moses as the two witnesses. At Christ's transfiguration, in preview of the Son of God coming in His royal splendor, it was Moses and Elijah who were with Him (Matt. 17:3). It is interesting to note (v. 1) that the transfiguration occurred "after 6

---

[36] Certainly, the world will be viewing this on news networks such as CNN, and it will be fulfilled before their very eyes.

[37] Tishri, or Ethanin, the 7th month of the Jewish religious year, the 1st month of the Jewish agricultural year.

days." This lines up with God coming, at His revelation, after six days of man's week.

Moses and Elijah represented not only the law and the prophets, but those who are to be resurrected[38] and translated as they were. (As Enoch never died, so shall some living today never die!)

In Psalm 45, the King is spoken of; toward the end of the chapter we see the royal bride in gold of Ophir (v. 9). Here we have the association of a king with a kingdom, and his bride with his wedding.

"All glorious is the princess within [her chamber]; her gown is interwoven with gold. In embroidered garments she is led to the king..." Psalm 45:13-14).

As we saw, the coronation of the King is at Rosh HaShanah. The wedding at the end of the age will logically occur during the week between Rosh HaShanah and Yom Kippur (10 days later). The wedding feast occurs soon after on the mountains of Israel (Isa. 25:6). Since the time in the wedding chamber is seven days (between Tishri 1 and Tishri 10), the wedding ceremony is easily placed during that time because everything has to be concluded by the 10th of Tishri (Yom Kippur). Let's examine Yom Kippur and see why.

Feast Of Yom Kippur

As Messiah's first coming (the suffering servant, a sacrifice on the cross) was on the 10th day of the first month

---

[38] God sent the archangel Michael to retrieve the body of Moses (Jude 9). Moses was resurrected so that the devil could not use his bones to set up a shrine for the Jews to worship, since Moses was thought of as being higher than the angels. This is why the author of Hebrews used the comparison of Jesus being greater than Moses (Heb. 3:3), after saying Christ was greater than the angels (Heb. 1:4).

of the religious calendar; His second coming, as the victorious king, will be on the 10th day of the seventh month of the religious calendar (first month of the civil calendar). This ties in with the former and latter rains mentioned in the book of Joel, among other places.

Yom Kippur is the Day of Atonement, and is considered the holiest day in the Jewish year. Every fifty years, there was a Jubilee on Yom Kippur. All debts were forgiven, all slaves or captives were released, and all lands were returned to their rightful owners (Lev. 25:8-55). These are types of works which are/will be fulfilled by Christ. For example, it is Christ who is, "to proclaim freedom for the captives...(Isa. 61:1)" In the year 2030 A.D., two days (2,000) years will have elapsed since His ascension. It will be the 40th Jubilee! Could there be a better day for the return of Christ than this day?

It was on Yom Kippur that blood offerings were performed by the high priest—one for his own sins, and the other for the sins of the Israelites. During a blood offering, the high priest wore linen garments. After the sacrifice, he changed into his regular priestly garments of glory and beauty and reappeared. He was in his priestly garments when he came out of the tent of meeting and sacrificed an offering by fire. The details of this are found in Leviticus 16.

The Lord instructed the Israelites to do this on the tenth day of the month of Tishri, "...*because on this day atonement will be made for you, to cleanse you*" (Lev. 16:30). For this reason Yom Kippur would also be known as the Day of Redemption. It is at this time that the Great Trumpet will be blown, to seal the final fate of those upon the earth.

This festival prophesies the literal, physical second

coming of Messiah, which will be the end! The different parts of the ceremony of Yom Kippur foretell events that will occur on that day.

The *first time the Messiah came He wore His* "linen garments," that is, He did not wear His garments of beauty or splendor:

"He grew up before him like a tender shoot, and like a root out of dry ground. He had no beauty or majesty to attract us to him, nothing in his appearance that we should desire him" (Isa. 53:2).

"Who, being in very nature God, did not consider equality with God something to be grasped, but made himself nothing, taking the very nature of a servant, being made in human likeness. And being found in appearance as a man, he humbled himself and became obedient to death; even death on a cross" (Phil. 2:6-8).

"…God did by sending his own Son in the likeness of sinful man to be a sin offering" (Rom. 8:3).

The Messiah Priest, at His first coming, offered His own blood at the Passover feast so that all who believe in His offering could be atoned (redeemed or saved) from their sins. The Messiah King, at His second coming, will offer His rejectors' blood at Yom Kippur so that all who didn't believe in His sin offering will find their reward!

This future blood offering will be at the Revelation of the Messiah on the Mount of Olives, in the vicinity of Bethany, from where He ascended:

"How beautiful on the mountains…; When the Lord returns to Zion, they will see it with their own eyes…and all the ends of the earth will see the salvation of our God" (Isa. 52:7-8, 10).

It is interesting to note that in Isaiah 12:2, the Lord, Jehovah, tells us, "The Lord has become my salvation." The Hebrew word for salvation in this usage is Yeshuwah. In Hebrew, it is literally translated, Jehovah's Salvation. In English, this is literally translated, Jehovah has become my Jesus!

---

*"See, my servant will act wisely; he will be raised and lifted up and highly exalted. Just as there were many who were appalled at him; his appearance was so disfigured beyond that of any man and his form marred beyond human likeness; so will he **sprinkle** many nations, and kings will shut their mouths because of him. For what they were not told, they will see, and what they have not heard, they will understand"* (Isa. 52:13-15).

We should understand that this sprinkling that is to occur at this future Yom Kippur is actually a great blood bath. Just as the Messiah was disfigured and marred and went through His own blood bath, so will His rejectors:

"They were trampled in the winepress outside the city, and blood flowed out of the press, rising as high as the horses' bridles for a distance of 1,600 stadia" (Rev. 14:20).

Sixteen hundred stadia is 180 miles—this will certainly be the largest blood offering/blood bath of all times! (see also "Grapes of Wrath" in chapter Six).

Azazel—The Demon Goat

During the ritual ceremony of Yom Kippur, there was present a goat known as the scapegoat or azazel. It signified the "goat of departure"; azaz means hardened or impudent. The azazel was bound and cast to his death from Mount Tzok (Mount Azazel) located about twelve miles from Jerusalem. The name Azazel is used by the Arabs to mean "evil demon." This demon goat represented the false god or false messiah (Satan or the Antichrist) and in perfect parallel will be either bound in Hades and/or cast alive into the Lake of Fire (respectively), on the last Yom Kippur (Rev. 20:2; 19:19-20).

Yom Kippur—Doomsday

On Yom Kippur, at a location between the porch and the altar, the high priest slew a bull during the ceremony. Joel, the prophet, speaks of the coming of the Messiah at the time of this ceremony.

"Blow the trumpet in Zion, declare a holy fast, call a sacred assembly. Gather the people, consecrate the assembly; bring together the elders, gather the children, those nursing at the breast. Let the bridegroom leave his room and the bride her chamber. Let the priests, who minister before the Lord, weep between the temple porch and the altar" (Joel 2:15-17).

The declared fast must be at Yom Kippur. It is the only festival that is a fast, the only one that is a solemn festival, and the only one that takes place between the porch and the altar!

The picture we have is a cry to the Messiah to come and end the persecution by the Antichrist and his armies. It also shows the bride coming back to the earth with the Messiah after the wedding ceremony in heaven.

Other passages, symbols, and visions also point to this Day of Atonement as being Doomsday:

"Listen, O high priest Joshua and your associates seated before you, who are men symbolic of things to come: I am going to bring my servant, the Branch...and I will remove the sin of this land in a single day" (Zech. 3:8-9).

This day is associated with Jehovah showing Himself

as the Messiah whom they pierced. It is also known as that day or the Day of the Lord.

"They will look on me, the one they have pierced..." Zech. 12:10).

"On that day a fountain will be opened to the house of David and to the inhabitants of Jerusalem to cleanse them from sin and impurity" (Zech. 13:1).

Lights Going On and Off

The day of Yom Kippur will be the day the Lord reveals Himself on the Mount of Olives.

At noontime, on that day of this religious feast, the sun will go out, and mourning and weeping will start:

"'In that day,' declares the Sovereign Lord, 'I will make the sun go down at noon and darken the earth in broad daylight. I will turn your religious feasts into mourning and all your singing into weeping. I will make that time like mourning for an only son and the end of it like a bitter day'" (Amos 8:9-10).

However, when the evening comes (6:00 p.m.) on this conclusive Yom Kippur, there will be light:

"Then the Lord will go out and fight against those nations, as he fights in the day of battle. On that day his feet will stand on the Mount of Olives, east of Jerusalem...the Lord my God will come, and all the holy ones with him. On that day there will be no light, no cold or frost. It will be a unique day, without daytime or nighttime—a day known to the Lord. When evening comes, there will be light" (Zech. 14:3-7).

After the bright noon sun goes out, the light is turned on, at 6:00 p.m. (Zech. 14:7). All will witness the terror of the Glory of God—Jesus Christ in His eminent glory!

"In the evening, sudden terror! Before the morning, they are gone" (Isa. 17:14)!

The prophet Ezekiel had no less of a vision for Yom

Kippur, "*At the beginning of the year, on the tenth of the month...*" (Ezek. 40:1). (This is Tishri 10.)

"*In visions of God he took me to the land of Israel...and I saw a man whose appearance was like bronze*" (Ezek. 40:2-3).

This is the same vision the Apostle John saw when he wrote the Book of Revelation—a vision he saw through the Holy Spirit on the Lord's Day (Rev 1:10). John saw this same man, who no doubt is Jesus Christ.

"*I turned around to see the voice that was speaking to me. And when I turned I saw...someone 'like a son of man,' dressed in a robe reaching down to his feet and with a golden sash around his chest. His head and hair were white like wool, as white as snow, and his eyes were like blazing fire. His feet were like bronze glowing in a furnace, and his voice was like the sound of rushing waters... His face was like the sun shining in all its brilliance*" (Rev. 1:12-16).

This compares to what Daniel the prophet saw in the 10th chapter of Daniel (v. 6), and in a vision of the Ancient of Days in the 7th chapter of Daniel (v. 9). Note that in verse 11, one like a son of man destroyed a beast (the Antichrist) and threw him into the blazing fire (the Lake of Fire).

The Omega is also seen by Daniel in a vision:

"*As I looked, thrones were set in place, and the Ancient of Days took his seat. His clothing was as white as snow [purity]; the hair of his head was white like wool [wisdom]. His throne was flaming with fire [authority], and its wheels were all ablaze [judgement]. A river of fire was flowing, coming out from before him. Thousands upon thousands attended him; ten thousand times' ten thousand stood before him. The court was seated, and the books were opened*" (Dan. 7:9-10).

Later, in the vision that Ezekiel had on Tishri 10,

where he saw the Man whose appearance was like bronze, he defines Him as the Glory of God.

"And I saw the glory of the God of Israel coming from the east. His voice was like the roar of rushing waters, and the land was radiant with his glory" (Ezek. 43:2).

This is unmistakably The End Himself!

Yom Kippur Dates Trumpet Woes

The seventh trumpet sounds as the kingdom of the world becomes the kingdom of the Lord (Rev. 11:15), and the King is crowned at Rosh HaShanah; thus all seven bowls making up the seventh trumpet occur in the last 10 days!

The seventh bowl brings lightning, thunder, severe earthquakes, sinking of islands and mountains, and giant hailstones (Rev. 16:18-21). The Lord's return is associated with these same elements (Psalm 18:9-12; 97:4, 5). Therefore, the seventh bowl is at the return of the Lord, on Yom Kippur, on that day, the end day!

The fifth and sixth trumpets in the book of Revelation are also known as the first and second woes. The fifth trumpet lasts five months (Rev. 9:5), followed by the sixth trumpet which lasts thirteen months (Rev. 9:15). This time period involves the great war, that if not stopped by Christ, would bring an end to all human flesh (Matt. 24:22)—instead of just one-third of mankind (Rev. 9:18)! Therefore, these woes begin eighteen months before the end at Yom Kippur, which dates them as beginning two years after the abomination of desolation—which occurs in the middle of the tribulation— close to or at the Jewish Passover. See Appendix , Fig. I.

Just as Joshua came into Jericho on the seventh day after the trumpets were blown, so Yeshua will come to

Jerusalem on the seventh day after the trumpets are blown.

At the next feast, the believers are gathered in Jerusalem to enjoy and to celebrate the Messiah's victory at the Feast of Sukkot (the Feast of Tabernacles).

Feast Of Tabernacles

The Feast of Tabernacles portrays a joyful time, namely the Messianic Kingdom. It was a harvest celebration observed after the last harvest of the year, from Tishri 15-22. This feast began with a sacred assembly, and after a week, was followed by a second, sacred assembly.

The feast is a memorial for Israel, both pointing back to Egypt and forward to their Millennial Rest; as the seventh day of the week is a sabbath or rest. The seventh religious month for Israel typifies a period of rest. At "the end," this sacred assembly begins fulfillment in a sabbatic rest. This sabbatic rest will be the promised time of refreshing—the 1,000-year day known as the Millennium. The second, sacred assembly on the eighth day represents the time when the New Jerusalem will be placed upon the earth. This will take place after a final cleansing and purification of the earth; involving the "melting" and reconstitution of the earth (2 Pet. 3:12-13). Finally, God will place His tabernacle (the New Jerusalem) on the earth and will then "tabernacle" (dwell) with man as He did during the first days of Adam (the first man). This will be fulfilled after the Millennium is over.

"I saw the Holy City, the new Jerusalem, coming down out of heaven from God, prepared as a bride beautifully dressed for her husband. And I heard a loud voice from the throne saying, 'Now the dwelling [tabernacle] of God is with men, and he will live with them. They will be his people, and God himself will be with them and be their God'" (Rev. 21:2-3).

Since God's tabernacle doesn't touch the earth until

the final cleansing after the Millennium, it must be suspended somewhere above the earth until then, presumably while it is "under construction." This is the place that Jesus went to prepare for His bride (John 14:2). Ezekiel also speaks of that future time when God's sanctuary (dwelling place or tabernacle) will be among them forever (Ezek. 37:27-28).

As we can see, it will take 1,000 years to fulfill all of this typical prophecy. But there are even more themes, shown in the way the Jews have celebrated this festival, that will be fulfilled at the beginning of the Millennium.

Water and Wind

During the historical celebration of the festival, some priests would go through the Water Gate of the Temple, and some priests would go through the Eastern Gate of the Temple. The first group would retrieve water from the Pool of Siloam, known as "living water" (as opposed to water that was stagnant and contained bacteria, as in a cistern). The second group would go to the Valley of the Motza and cut down willow trees. The two groups would come back to the temple simultaneously. As the second group came in they waved their willow branches, producing the effect of a rushing wind, which symbolized the coming of the Holy Spirit of God. They placed their willows at the base of the altar, forming a sukkah (booth or tabernacle) over its top. The high priest took the living water from the first group and poured it out over the altar. There was also a sacrifice. As all this was performed, the people sang Isaiah 12:3:[39]

---

[39] This picture of Jewish history is drawn from Joseph Good's book, Rosh HaShanah and the Messianic Kingdom to Come, Hatikva Ministries, Port Author, Texas; p. 45-46; used with permission.

"Therefore with joy shall you draw water out of the wells of salvation" (KJV).

This unique feast shows the post-judgement days (after the Tribulation), in which the Salvation has returned; the Water is Jesus, and the Wind is the Holy Spirit. The Feast of Tabernacles is the setting for the following prophecy:

"On the last and greatest day of the Feast, Jesus stood and said in a loud voice, `If anyone is thirsty, let him come to me and drink. Whoever believes in me, as the Scripture has said, streams of living water will flow from within him'" (John 7:37-38).

The only scripture Christ could be referring to is the above passage (Isaiah 12:3)—that the Jews sang at the end of the Feast of Tabernacles. Here Christ claims to be the Salvation or God, of which the Lord spoke in Isaiah 12:2. There it tells us that Jehovah has become our Yeshua or Jesus (salvation).

The prophet Joel speaks of the Spirit being poured out after God is in Israel:

"I am in Israel...the Lord your God" (Joel 2:27).

"And afterward, I will pour out my Spirit on all people. Your sons and daughters will prophesy, your old men will dream dreams, your young men will see visions" (Joel 2:28).

Isaiah shows this same pouring associated with physical and spiritual watering during the Millennium.

"For I will pour water on the thirsty land, and streams on the dry ground; I will pour out my Spirit on your offspring, and my blessing on your descendants" (Isa. 44:3).

Thus, at the beginning of the Millennium, after God returns to physically dwell in the presence of the Jews, He will pour out His Spirit upon all people. This is part of what the Feast of Tabernacles portrays. It also portrays a time of the presence of God's glory living among His people.

Israel & God's Glory in the Wilderness

The ceremony of living in temporary booths during the Feast of Tabernacles points to the time that Israel wandered in the wilderness (Lev. 23:43) living in tents. During this time, God lived with His people in a tent as well.

"Go and tell my servant David, 'This is what the Lord says: You are not the one to build me a house to dwell in. I have not dwelt in a house from the day I brought Israel up out of Egypt to this day. I have moved from one tent site to another, from one dwelling place to another'" (1 Chron. 17:4-5).

God's glory was present with the Israelites in the form of a white cloud. When the tabernacle or Tent of Meeting was dedicated, God's, *"...cloud covered the Tent of Meeting, and the glory of the Lord filled the tabernacle"* (Exod. 40:34).

"So the cloud of the Lord was over the tabernacle by day, and fire was in the cloud by night, in the sight of all the house of Israel during all their travels" (Exod. 40:38).

We are to understand that the cloud is intimately connected with and representative of the Glory of God (Exod. 13:20-21; 14:19; 16:10).

Angel of the Lord & Yeshua

In the above verses, the Glory of God in the form of a cloud is also associated with the Angel of the Lord (Exod. 14:19). Exodus 23:20-28 shows that this angel has the name of the Lord in Him, and was known as "my angel," "my terror," and "the hornet." The Angel of the Lord is first seen at Genesis 16:7, where He appears to Haggar and she later identifies Him as God (Gen. 16:13). The Angel of the Lord is shown to be God by Abraham (Gen. 22:11-16). This was after the Lord appeared to Abraham as a man (Gen. 18:2, 10, 13). The Angel of the Lord is also shown as the Lord (Gen. 22:15-16).

Clearly, in numerous passages, the Angel of the Lord is shown as God! Hosea 12:3-5 identifies the Man with whom Jacob wrestled as "the Angel" and "the Lord God Almighty." Jacob himself wanted to know His name, and knew he had seen God face to face after he had wrestled with Him all night. What these verses clearly show is that God appeared as the Angel of the Lord and as a man in the Old Testament.

The Man who appeared in the Old Testament was the Messiah. It should have been common knowledge that when God appeared in a human body—as a baby in a manger (1 Tim. 3:16)—He was the one from everlasting or the eternal one (see Micah 5:2, Psalm 90:2; and Psalm 93:2). Whenever the omnipresent God becomes visible, He appears as either an Angel or a Man. The Angel of the Lord was not seen during Messiah's time on earth because He was here in the flesh! He tabernacled or dwelt among people (John 1:14). The Angel of the Lord was the Christ when He was on the earth, from His birth as a baby in a manger, to His ascension. They are one and the same!

The scriptures tell us, *"No one has ever seen God, but God the only Son, who is at the Father's side, has made him known"* (John 1:18). It is clear from the passages just mentioned, that Abraham and others have both seen Jehovah God and spoken with Him. We can thus easily conclude from John 1:18 that the one seen by Abraham was God the only Son, or the pre-incarnate Messiah—known to us today as Jesus.

The fact that Jesus is God is clearly shown by John the Apostle. John quotes a passage (John 12:40) from the book of Isaiah (Isa. 6:10). This Isaiah passage comes just after a description of Jehovah:

"...I saw the LORD seated on a throne, high and exalted, and the train of his robe filled the temple. ...Holy, holy, holy is the LORD Almighty; the whole earth is full of his glory....my eyes have seen the King, the LORD Almighty" (Isa. 6:1, 3, 5).

In John's next passage, he states that Isaiah described Jesus, and spoke of Him:

"Isaiah said this because he saw Jesus' glory and spoke about him" (John 12:41).

Jehovah, the King, is known by Christians as Jesus, the coming King of Kings. Samson's father, Manoah, saw the Angel of the Lord and asked Him His name (as had Jacob). The Angel gave him His name in Hebrew, which interprets as "Wonderful." Later, Manoah stated that he had seen God (Judges 13:17-22). Isaiah 9:6 tells us that a Son is given (Son of God) and a child is born (Son of Man). This God-Man was to be born of a virgin (Isa. 7:14) and would be called Immanuel, which means "God with us." Several names are given in Isaiah 9:6; among them, Mighty God and Wonderful—the name the Angel of the Lord revealed to Manoah. This God-Man is the same Angel of the Lord. Exodus 23:21 informs us that Yahweh's (Jehovah's) name would be in Him. The angel's now common name is Yeshua (Yahweh saves); again, this is translated in English as Jesus!

The glory of the Lord comes together then as the Man with Abraham and Jacob (the pre-incarnate Messiah), the Angel of the Lord, and the Cloud (a pillar of fire by night), which remained with the Israelites throughout their 40 years of desert wandering. This same pillar of cloud and fire met Moses on Mount Sinai.

"When Moses went up on the mountain, the cloud covered it, and the glory of the Lord settled on Mount Sinai. For six days the cloud covered the mountain, and on the seventh

day the LORD called to Moses from within the cloud. To the Israelites the glory of the Lord looked like a consuming fire on top of the mountain" (Exod. 24:15-17).

This passage is a type of what will happen when the seventh day or the Millennial-Sabbath Day comes, for it was on the seventh day that Moses went up the mountain. Chapter 19 of Exodus provides us with several details. Israel was God's treasured possession (Deut. 7:6), and will be again (Matt. 13:44). Israel is to be a kingdom of priests (Exod. 19:6), after God descends to them for a final time at the end of the tribulation. This will be after two days (2,000 years) and at the beginning of the third day (Millennial Day) (Hosea 6:2), as typified in the book of Exodus: *"...and be ready by the third day, because on that day the Lord will come down..."* (Exod. 19:11).

"On the morning of the third day there was thunder and lightning, with a thick cloud over the mountain, and a very loud trumpet blast" (Exod. 19:16).

A Glorious Cloud To Return

As we will see in chapter six, "HOW," Exodus 19:16 typifies the Revelation of God (Christ) on Mount Zion. This cloud represents the believers of Christ who are in His tabernacle, the New Jerusalem, and which cloud will cover all of Israel during the Millennium, beginning on the morning of the third day. Let's examine the passages that show this.

The glory of the Lord that covered the mountain at Sinai looked to the Israelites to be a fire (Exod. 24:18). This is the same cloud by day and pillar of fire by night that led and protected the people of Israel (Exod. 13:21; Neh. 9:12). God commanded a sanctuary to be made so that He could have a place to dwell (tabernacle) among the Israelites (Exod. 25:8). Until then, the glorious cloud by day and fire by night was His dwelling place.

In the future, God will once again dwell in a glorious tabernacle. Jerusalem will be a peaceful abode, a tent that will not be moved (Isa. 33:20). The Lord tells us that in that day (the Millennial Day, after the fiery judgement of the Tribulation) the survivors will be recorded among the living (Isa. 4:2-4). He will again employ a protective, sheltering cloud, as He did during the wilderness wanderings.

"Then the LORD will create over all of Mount Zion and over those who assemble there a cloud of smoke by day and a glow of flaming fire by night; over all the glory will be a canopy. It will be a shelter and shade from the heat of the day, and a refuge and hiding place from the storm and rain" (Isa. 4:5-6).

The cloud enshrouds and is the Holy City, the New Jerusalem, which is adorned as a bride (Rev. 21:9-10). Its base is 1,400 miles square (Rev. 21:16). The glorious cloud of the Lord will cover all of the original royal grant to Abraham, which extends over to the Euphrates River in Iraq. All this belongs to Israel, and at long last, the Lord will claim it for them, never again to allow surrender to opposition!

We know that when Christ ascended into heaven He was accompanied by a cloud (Acts 1:9), and that when He returns, it will be in the same way (Acts 1:11; Matt. 24:30). This ascension was accompanied by captives who were *"led in his train,"* presumably from Hades (Psalm 68:18; Eph. 4:8). The cloud, then, is composed of spiritual beings! It shouldn't be a great surprise to learn that these clouds are composed of more than water vapor! Hebrews 12:1 speaks of a cloud of witnesses. The two witnesses in Rev. 11:12 will ascend in a cloud. The Mystery Church will translate and ascend to heaven to be in the clouds (composed of angels, past Old Testament Saints, and newly resurrected saints of the Church).

In clouds such as these are to be ten thousand times ten thousand (Rev. 5:11). Ten thousands will come with the Lord (Jude 14). God is to dwell at a mountain (Mt. Zion) and will come and make His sanctuary there. He will have there tens of thousands of "chariots" (Psalm 68:17). The clouds are His chariot (Psalm 104:3), and He will come again with them (Isa. 66:15; Hab. 3:8).

The glory of the Lord is to appear over Zion (Isa. 60:2) and there are to be those who *"fly along like clouds"* (Isa. 60:8).

Psalm 105:28 - 106:5 gives part of the past history of the Israelites, which will be repeated in the future tribulation, but ends in the joy of becoming God's inheritance. It speaks of plagues, a cloud for covering, waters gushing out of rocks, and glorying in God's inheritance.

Heavenly & Earthly Tabernacles

It is upon Mt. Zion where the heavenly beings are to dwell, in communication with the earth. This is what Peter anticipated. It was on a high mountain that the Lord showed His inner circle of people (Peter, James, and John) a preview of Himself coming in His regal splendor. Note that it was after six days, or on the seventh day. This further suggests the coming of the Lord on the beginning of the seventh or Sabbath-Millennial Day! With the Lord was Moses, a type of the resurrected saints, and Elijah, a type of the translated or raptured saints. A bright cloud developed there.

Peter said to Jesus, *"Lord, it is good for us to be here; if thou will, let us make here three tabernacles; one for thee, and one for Moses, and one for Elias"* (Matt. 17:4, KJV).

What Peter desired was the dwelling of heavenly people in communion with the earth. It will be this way, beginning at the Millennial Day. It appears that the first resident association of heavenly with earthly will be at the marriage feast of the Lamb, when Christ and His bride entertain wedding guests at the beginning of the Millennium—at the first Feast of Tabernacles immediately following the Revelation of Jesus Christ on Yom Kippur.

"On this mountain the Lord Almighty will prepare a feast of rich food for all peoples, a banquet of aged wine; the best of meats and the finest of wines" (Isa. 25:6).

In this cloud over Zion will the Lord dwell in His sanctuary and be among the people of the earth, not only during the Millennium but forever.

"'...I will put my sanctuary among them forever. My dwelling place will be with them; I will be their God, and they will be my people. Then the nations will know that I the Lord make Israel holy, when my sanctuary is among them forever'" (Ezek. 37:26-28).

Feast Of Hanukkah

Hanukkah is also called the Festival of Lights, and the Feast of Dedication. This is celebrated by the Jews on the 25th day of the month of Kislev[40] for eight days. Readers should note that this is not one of the seven festivals described in the Old Testament. It's not there because the event that it commemorates occurred during the inter-testament period (between the Old and New Testament), during the 400 years of God's silence.

Between the writings of the Old and New Testament, certain prophesied events of Daniel occurred. Alexander

---

[40] Kislev, or Chisleu, the 9th month of the Jewish religious year.

the Great had expanded the Greek Empire and died, leaving his empire divided among four generals. One division, the Seleucid dynasty of Syria, came to rule over Jerusalem and Judea. A beast named Antiochus Epiphanes (described in the book of Daniel) instituted a reign of terror. He erected a statue of Zeus (a Greek god) bearing his own facial features and slaughtered a sow on the altar in the temple at Jerusalem.

Later, Judah Maccabees and others won independence for the Jews in 165 B.C. The temple was rededicated after the idols were crushed, and things were repaired and cleaned. The last thing to do was to relight the seven-branched menorah. Pure oil had to be used, but there was only enough for one day, and it required eight days to make more. However, the pure oil on hand burned for eight days rather than just one. In celebration of this rededication of the Temple, candles are lighted each year, for eight consecutive days. On the first night this blessing is chanted:

"Blessed are You, O Lord our God, King of the universe, who has granted us life, and has preserved us, and has enabled us to this season."[41]

The Abomination

The beast Antiochus Epiphanes is a type of the future beast, the Antichrist. Just as the first beast erected an abomination (or a statue) to himself and did away with the worship of God, so will the second, future beast (Rev. 13:14-15). However, just as Judah gained freedom for the Jews, and illuminated the Temple with his candles; the

---

[41] "The Gates Magazine", Fall 1992, Hatikvah Ministries, Port Arthur, Texas, p. 22; used with permission.

Lion of the tribe of Judah, Jesus, will obtain eternal freedom, and illuminate the Millennial Temple with His Glory. The future celebration of the rededication and the start of a new era will occur after much mourning and cleaning up in the future on the very same day, Kislev 25. Let's examine scriptures that show us this event.

"The man clothed in linen, who was above the waters of the river, lifted his right hand and his left hand toward heaven, and I heard him swear by him who lives forever, saying, 'It will be for a time, times and half a time. When the power of the holy people has been finally broken, all these things will be completed'" (Dan. 12:7).

The Son of God said it would be for a year, two years and half a year. In God's prophetic year of 360 days, this is 1,260 days. 1,260 days before the end, on Yom Kippur (Tishri 10), is the period of the last half of the tribulation (see timeline illustration in Appendix , Fig. I). This makes the future abomination by the Antichrist at the time of the Passover. It will be the time spoken of by Christ, when the abomination is set up, and great tribulation begins:

"When ye therefore shall see the abomination of desolation, spoken of by Daniel the prophet, stand in the holy place, (whoso readeth, let him understand:) Then let them which be in Judaea flee into the mountains: For then shall be great tribulation, such as was not since the beginning of the world to this time, no, nor ever shall be" (Matt. 24:15-16, 21, KJV).

This abomination is probably something like a "flesh" covered robotic statue of the beast, as the culmination of man's most innovative and creative technological wizardry. It seems as if this "robotic creature" may be "booted up," or make his appearance, during the same week that Christ rode into Jerusalem on a donkey, bringing peace and salvation (Zech. 9:9-10; Matt. 21:5).

Christ was crucified—rejected—on the cross. He said

that another would come in his own name but that he would be accepted (John 5:43). Perhaps he, the Antichrist, "arrives" on this day as well, but his mission is to break the peace, and to bring war and damnation (Dan. 9:27).

It is possible that the Antichrist may also levitate himself or his abomination on a cloud in the temple according to Daniel 9:27. Other passages, such as Revelations 13:12, appear to show the beast being healed of a fatal wound. Most probably he will be slain on Nisan 14 and will rise from the dead three days later, in order to completely imitate Christ and thus deceive the masses.

At the end of the book of Daniel we are given more numbers, which take us days past the tribulation.

"From the time that the daily sacrifice is abolished and the abomination that causes desolation is set up, there will be 1,290 days. Blessed is the one who waits for and reaches the end of the 1,335 days" (Dan. 12:11-12).

30 & 75 Days Past The End

The passage in Daniel 12:11 gives us 1,290 days from the abomination, or 30 days past the Revelation of God as Jesus Christ on Yom Kippur, Tishri 10.

Thirty days was the traditional time of Jewish mourning, as seen in the way they mourned for the deliverer of Israel, Moses:

"The Israelites grieved for Moses in the plains of Moab thirty days, until the time of weeping and mourning was over" (Deut. 34:8).

In the same way, they will also mourn for the deliverer of Israel, Christ.

"They will look on me, the one they have pierced, and they will mourn for him as one mourns for an only child, and grieve bitterly for him as one grieves for a firstborn son" (Zech. 12:10).

Moses wrote that a prophet like himself would be raised up later (Deut. 18:15), and Peter confirmed to Jews that Christ was the One of whom Moses spoke (Acts 3:22). Peter said the Jews should repent and receive the times of refreshing; the Millennial Day (Acts 3:19). This the Jews will do at the end—everyone who is left at the end of the tribulation will be or will become "Jews for Jesus." The rest will have been killed (Zech. 13:8). They will do this because they will not see their Messiah (Christ) again until they say, *"Blessed is he who comes in the name of the Lord"* (Matt. 23:39).

The 45 days remaining (the days left to reach the 1,335 days of Dan 12:12) is for the judgement (or continuing judgement) of the sheep and goats. Those who will be blessed will be those who have the privilege of entering into the Millennial Kingdom. *"He will put the sheep on his right and the goats on his left. Then the King will say to those on his right, 'Come, you who are blessed by my Father; take your inheritance, the kingdom prepared for you since the creation of the world'"* (Matt. 25:34).

It is at this same time that the weeds or goats, those people who have chosen darkness (sin and evil), are cast into the fire of Hades.

The goats are those who do not hear His voice and do not receive eternal life. This is what Jesus said when He spoke to goats on the very day of this feast (John 10:22-28)! It will be on this day that the judgement of the sheep and goats will end.

"As the weeds are pulled up and burned in the fire, so it will be at the end of the age. The Son of Man will send out his angels, and they will weed out of his kingdom everything that causes sin and all who do evil. They will throw them into the fiery furnace, where there will be weeping and gnashing of teeth. Then the righteous will shine like the sun in the kingdom of their Father" (Matt. 13:40-43).

This takes us back to the parallel passage in Daniel:

"Those who are wise will shine like the brightness of the heavens, and those who lead many to righteousness, like the stars for ever and ever. But you, Daniel, close up and seal the words of the scroll until the time of the end. Many will go here and there to increase knowledge" (Dan. 12:3-4).

As we saw, the 1,260 days run out at Yom Kippur, and 30 additional days are allotted for the mourning, to bring us to the 1,290th day. Then, the additional 45 days brings us to the 1,335th day. On the Jewish calendar, this will bring us to Kislev 25—the feast at Hanukkah. At least four times, God has used Kislev 24 as an important date in past Jewish history. In 520 B.C., the foundations of the temple were laid. In 168 B.C., the temple sacrifice was abolished. In 165 B.C., the temple was recaptured and cleansed. In 1917 A.D., Jerusalem was freed from Turkish rule. It will be in the future, on Hanukkah, that once again, we who will be there, will celebrate God's cleansing—on the very day the celebration of the Temple rededication was inaugurated.

Those who reach the 24th day of Kislev will be blessed! The prophet Haggai also supports this day as the day when all present upon the earth are blessed by being allowed to enter the millenium: "From this day on, from this twenty-fourth day of the ninth month... From this day on I will bless you" (Haggai 2:18-19).

SUMMARY

God has informed us that the End of the age will come in relation to His dealing with the nation of Israel. The Omega (Messiah) stated emphatically that no one at the time He was on the earth knew when the end would come, including Himself. However, He did not say that no one would know at a later time. Just days later, He Himself knew after He again took on the fullness of the Glory of God with all power and all knowledge.

The Bible shows that man's day will end on the same day that the Day of the Lord begins, when He has promised to restore Israel. This time of restoration brings peace, and the general times of refreshing, ruled over by the King of kings (the Prince of Peace). It is immediately after the end day (at that day) that Israel's restoration takes place (Amos 9:11).

God said that He would go back to His place until the Jews admitted their guilt (Hos. 5:15). He later informed us by His own mouth that He was leaving and that Israel's house would be desolate (Matt. 24:2). He will be away for two days, and the third day will become the restoration day (Hos. 6:2). As we saw, the restoration day (the Millennial Day, or Day of the Lord) is going to be 1,000 years long, thus the other two days (being in the same context of time) will be 2,000 years. Therefore, the third day will begin 2,000 years after His leaving.

We determined the year directly from written prophecy. We determined the day from typical prophecy. At Yom Kippur, the High Priest in his linen garments shed blood and made atonement for the people. He then reappeared from the Holy of Holies (within the temple) dressed in his garments of glory and beauty. He thus revealed himself, showing that his blood offering had been accepted, and that the people had been "saved." This typifies the day on which Jesus, the High Priest—Messiah Ben Joseph—who was made in the likeness of sinful man (linen garments), shed His own blood, and made atonement for all believers. As Messiah, the King of Kings—Messiah Ben David—He will soon come out of the Holy of Holies in Heaven, fully dressed in all His glory and regal splendor.

The King of Kings and Lord of Lords will reveal Himself, showing that His blood offering was accepted, and that Israel has been saved—on the Day of Redemption or Day of Atonement (Yom Kippur).

By knowing the date of Yom Kippur, one can work backwards through time to know when other events, which also have specific time periods, will occur. For example, the fifth trumpet begins eighteen months earlier, which starts a great war. These dates can all be checked more precisely in the future, once the abomination of desolation occurs. For it is 1,260 days after the abomination that the end occurs.

CHAPTER 4

WHERE DOES IT END?

Judgement Over All the Earth

M any contend that the judgements will only involve the area of the Middle East. Scripture shows us that, while they begin there, they will spread to the rest of the world. With all the talk of our global village, and the ever increasing, intertwining, and interconnection of social, political, and economic territories, common sense dictates that all of mankind, especially at a time further in the future, will be subject to the influence of God's judgements.

Jerusalem, Israel, and the Middle East will be the epi-center of this future tribulation, and will experience the greatest conflagration of the dominion of the Antichrist. This time of tribulation is in fulfillment of what was written long ago—by the Jews and for the Jews (Luke 21:22-23).

It is a scriptural principle that judgement begins at the house of God (1 Pet. 4:17). Jeremiah the prophet informs us of God's own words: *"'See, I am beginning to bring disaster on* the city that bears my Name, and will you indeed go unpunished? You will not go unpunished, for I am calling down a sword upon all who live on the earth,' declares the Lord Almighty. Now prophesy all these words against them and say to them: 'The LORD will roar from on high; he will thunder from his holy dwelling and roar mightily against his land. He will shout like those who tread the grapes, shout against all who live on the earth. The tumult will resound to the ends of the earth, for the Lord will bring charges against the nations; he will bring judgment on all mankind and put the wicked to the sword,' declares the Lord" (Jer. 25:29-31).

In the past, this referred to God's judgement executed by the then world ruler of Babylon, Nebuchadnezzar. But as all will soon see, a future world ruler of Babylon, the Antichrist, will come, and a future judgement will encompass the earth. (Israel's future restoration will come after this fearful future judgement.)

"'In **that day**,' declares the Lord Almighty, 'I will break the yoke off their necks and will tear off their bonds; no longer will foreigners enslave them. Instead, they will serve the Lord their God and David their king, whom I will raise up for them. I will surely save you out of a distant place... Though I completely destroy all the nations among which I scatter you, I will not completely destroy you" (Jer. 30:8, 9, 10, 11).

This worldwide judgement (among all the nations where the Jews have been scattered) is to take place on "that day." This is yet future, attested to by the fact that King David will be resurrected, as mentioned in the above portion of prophecy (Jer. 30:9).

This future tribulation judgement is seen as covering a third of the earth and a third of the sea (Rev. 8:7-8). The sixth trumpet judgement kills a third of mankind (Rev. 9:15). During the seventh trumpet's vial or bowl judgements, all of the seas are stricken, and every living thing in them dies (Rev. 16:3). Later, the sun becomes so intense that people are scorched with fire (Rev. 16:8). Thus, these judgements are worldwide.[42]

JUDGEMENT BEGINS AT THE FUTURE TEMPLE

The prophet Ezekiel had a vision of an abominable idol in the temple of God (Ezek. 8:3). (See "The Abomination," Chapter Three, for details.) This will be the temple occupation by the Antichrist during the tribulation. After certain servants of God receive seals in their foreheads (the future 144,000 of Rev. 7:3), the Glory of the God of Israel—Jesus Christ, the former Angel of the Lord—begins judgement at the middle of the tribulation and at the temple sanctuary. Here are Jesus' words for the future:

"Follow him through the city and kill, without showing pity or compassion. Slaughter old men, young men and maidens, women and children, but do not touch anyone who has the mark. Begin at my sanctuary. Defile the temple and fill the courts with the slain. Go!" (Ezek. 9:5-7).

This is the same Jesus who warned everyone that when they saw this abominable idol they should flee (Matt. 24:15-16). This is where the end shall begin—at the temple in Jerusalem. It will begin in the middle of the seven-year peace treaty, which will be broken by the one Ezekiel's abominable idol portrays (Antichrist)—the one who will probably rise from the dead in the month of Nisan, 3-1/2 years before the end at Jerusalem, on Tishri 10.

This picture of Jesus—a picture of one to be feared by the unsaved—hardly fits the popularized version of which

---

[42] A worldwide judgement is further reinforced by the fact that there is only one sun and it certainly reaches all of the earth.

we hear so much today. Today, He is frequently portrayed only as the gentle, compassionate man or teacher of long ago, a man who gathered children around himself, and who didn't even defend Himself throughout His own mock trial and crucifixion. Yet, He is and was the great I AM, "...*the same yesterday and today and forever*" (Heb. 13:8). The unsaved would do well to take heed, and begin to plant wisdom by gaining a fear of the living Lord (Prov. 9:10)!

The prophet Ezekiel saw an angel going ahead of the slaughter; the same angel of Revelation 7:2. He is placing the seal of God in their foreheads, which must take place before anything on the earth may be harmed. It appears that these 144,000 sealed ones will have an important ministry of witnessing to their fellow Jews about the Messiah, and will need special protection to do so. This new revival in the middle of the seven-year tribulation is the answer to the prophet Habakkuk who petitioned, "*O Lord, revive thy work in the midst of the years, in the midst of the years make known; in wrath remember mercy*" (Hab. 3:2, KJV).

The 144,000 sealed ones are to be protected from the physical judgements that begin at the temple. The future Antichrist (who will perhaps be the one to help with the rebuilding of the temple on Mt. Moriah) will have been allowing a reinstitution of the Jews' ancient worship, including sacrificial offerings. As a result, many Jews will have gathered at the temple. In the book of Revelation, the Apostle John was given a measuring rod with which to measure (that is to judge). John represents the redeemed in Christ.[43] He prophesied before many peoples, nations, languages, and kings (Rev. 10:11), but it was at the temple that his prophesied judgements would begin, prior to being executed throughout the world.

---

[43] As joint heirs with Christ, all of the redeemed will participate at some point with administering judgement.

JUDGEMENT OF AND BY CHRISTIANS

We who are in Christ are to judge the world (1 Cor. 6:2)—after we have been judged ourselves at the judgement seat of Christ (for our works). God always judges His own people first, and then His enemies.

The sacrifices at the future temple of the tribulation will be based on a confirmed covenant made by the false messiah. The sacrificial altar there will be an insult to the Lamb of God, who had offered His own blood as the perfect, final sacrifice (Heb. 10:10). The worshipers there profess to honor God, yet reject Christ.

John defines them as liars: *"Who is the liar? It is the man who denies that Jesus is the Christ. Such a man is the Antichrist; he denies the Father and the Son. No one who denies the Son has the Father; whoever acknowledges the Son has the Father also"* (1 John 2:22-23).

God is going to send these liars a powerful delusion through displays of "miracles, signs, and wonders." Some will believe the Lie (Antichrist) and will be condemned because they did not believe the Truth (Jesus Christ), but delighted in wickedness (2 Thess. 2:9-12). Those who worship the beast and his abominable image, or receive his mark or number, will drink of the wine of God's fury and be tormented for ever and ever (Rev. 14:9-11). The beginning of the end is at Jerusalem, but by the end of the tribulation 3-1/2 years later, the world will be engulfed in the wrath of God.

A KING FROM IRAQ

Much of Daniel 11 is hard to interpret, for it seems both historical and prophetical. This author believes that one time frame is possibly just before the middle of the seven-year peace covenant, after which time a ruler of the

Southern area[44] will engage the Antichrist in battle. The "king of the South" will most likely be the ruler over Egypt, Libya, and Ethiopia. He will lead an assault on the Antichrist, "King of the North" who thinks he is the king of kings. *"At the time of the end the king of the South will engage him in battle, and the king of the North will storm out against him with chariots and cavalry and a great fleet of ships"* (Dan. 11:40).

This "king of the North," the Antichrist, will have to leave his capital in Babylon (in present day Iraq) to subdue the king of the South. This will be the first of three kings, who will be subdued (Dan. 7:24). Parallel passage "types" in Jeremiah 46 appear to offer additional detail.

GOD THE MESSIAH CRUSHES JORDAN

In Daniel 11:41, we see that Edom, Moab, and Ammon (which is occupied by modern day Jordan) escape out of the Antichrist's hand. Perhaps because the Jordanian Arabs are much like him, they join the destroyer in an alliance. *"'Come,' they say, 'let us destroy them as a nation, that the name of Israel be remembered no more.' With one mind they plot together; they form an alliance against you; the tents of Edom and the Ishmaelites, of Moab and the Hagrites, Gebal, Ammon and Amalek"* (Psalm 83:4-7).

In reality, the Jordanians are not spared just because it was in the destroyer's mind to do so (for he is only a tool under God's sovereignty), but because God Himself— Jesus Christ—will at His return be the sole judge of these

[44] It appears that this area will be part of a 10-king area comprised of the revised Roman, Grecian, Medo-Persian, and Babylonian empires, corresponding to the ten toes of the interpreted image in Daniel 2:42.

Jordanians. Jesus Christ, who is, "the Root and the Offspring of David, and the bright Morning Star (Rev. 22:16)," will slaughter them Himself for destroying His people, the Jews; at the same time He will fulfill this prophecy:

"A star will come out of Jacob; a scepter will rise out of Israel. He will crush the foreheads of Moab, the skulls of all the sons of Sheth. Edom will be conquered; Seir, his enemy, will be conquered, but Israel will grow strong" (Num. 24:17-18).

Christ, the bright Morning Star, who comes out of Jacob (or from his portion) is called The Lord Almighty: *"He who is the Portion of Jacob is not like these, for he is the Maker of all things, including the tribe of his inheritance; the Lord Almighty is his name"* (Jer. 51:19).

Here we see that the Messiah, who would be descended from Jacob, is the Creator (Maker)—God Almighty! He is, the Holy One of Jacob…the God of Israel (Isa. 29:23).

We saw in the first chapter, "WHO is The End?" that the Messiah is both the Alpha, or Beginning, and the Omega, or End. We know from the first verse in Genesis, *"In the beginning God created the heavens and the earth,"* that the Creator is indeed the Alpha. Since the Messiah is the Beginning or Alpha, the Messiah is the Creator—the Messiah is God Almighty!

BABYLON

Ancient Babylon will be rebuilt in modern day Iraq, and will be the location of many of the important events of the end time. The book of Revelation describes both Babylon and her king.

"The beast, which you saw, once was, now is not, and will come up out of the Abyss and go to his destruction" (Rev. 17:8).

The Antichrist will rise up in tandem with the future, rebuilt city of Babylon. This passage refers to both the Emperor and his Empire. The symbolic beast has symbolic heads (Rev 17:9), which we are told represent "kings" (people) and "hills" (places). Many commentators believe the city to be revived is Rome, but Rome was present in John's day and can therefore not be described as "now is not."

In his book, The Revelation Record, Dr. Henry Morris interprets the passage below, the understanding of which requires a mind of wisdom (Rev. 17:9): *"Five have fallen, one is, the other has not come; but when he does come, he must remain for a little while"* (Rev. 17:10).

Dr. Morris identifies Babylonia, Egypt, Assyria, Persia, and Greece as the five that have fallen; and Rome as the one that is in John's day. He adds that the seventh kingdom will be composed of a ten-kingdom alliance. This alliance will not be that of the European Union or European Economic Community, which is proposed by many, for much of it is outside the old Greco-Roman Empire. The ten-kingdom alliance will be located within the "legs" of the eastern and western division of the old Roman Empire, and under the waist of the Grecian—just as the toes of Daniel's image are located on each leg, and under his waist. (See Appendix, Fig. II for a map of the Old Roman Empire.)

Morris states that the seventh kingdom, composed of the ten-kingdom alliance, will not last long, that it will probably exist for only the first 3-1/2 years of the first half of the tribulation. Thus, around the midpoint of the tribulation, the eighth king (the Antichrist) who will be of the seventh kingdom, the ten-kingdom United Nation Alliance (Rev 17:11), will receive power and strength (Rev 17:13). By this time, the city of Babylon will have been rebuilt and will host this new "United Nations" headquarters.[45] Due to its being near the geographic center of the world, it will become the new world trade center—the commercial capital of the globe. The prophet Zechariah informs us of this in his vision (5:5-11). In this vision, the woman represents the idolatry of mammon—the love of which is the root of all evil (1 Tim. 6:10). The basket or ephah was the primary volumetric measure used in trading; the Land of Shinar is Babylon. Zechariah thus informs us that those who worship money and trading will move to Babylon.

Babylon, with all this political power, will be the economic powerhouse of the world. Financiers, bankers, traders, and others involved in commerce, with offices in such major cities as New York, London, and Tokyo, will be well represented there. Those particularly involved in cargo shipping, such as sea captains, and administrators of port authorities will regularly trade with her (Rev. 18:17).

This author, who has some limited experience in international trade and warehousing, sees Babylon becoming a Free Trade Zone—where one will be able to import and export without taxation. The number of warehouses and refineries along the Euphrates will be even greater than the number of oil wells there, pumping their relentless rivers of black gold.

---

[45] Perhaps Iraq will continue to be a threat to the community of nations, and the present United Nations will gain control over it, or at least over Babylon. At such time, they will declare the area of Babylon an "international embassy," a "Vatican City," which will belong equally to all. If this happens, it could occur before the appearance of the Antichrist.

Many will become incredibly wealthy, but their wealth will not preserve them when the entire city of Babylon sinks in the coming earthquake!

ARMAGEDDON

At the very end of the tribulation, the long awaited battle of Armageddon takes place. The word "Armageddon" comes from the Hebrew Har-megiddo, or "Mountain of Megiddo." Mount Megiddo is about sixty miles north of Jerusalem. It overlooks the plain of Megiddo on the west and the plain of Esdraelon (or valley of Jezreel) on the northeast. It is to these plains that multitudes will gather for an assault at Jerusalem. (Multitudes would not be necessary just to capture the Jews who will still be left there at that time.)

Apparently, someone or something has to attract them. This will be accomplished by Satan, the Antichrist, and the False Prophet (Rev. 16:12, 19:19-20; 20:1-2) displaying their supernatural powers. Also, from Revelation 14:1, it will be known that the Lamb will appear soon and with Him 144,000 saints. Surely, some will have counted down 1,260 days from the abomination of desolation and will knowingly be preparing for battle against Christ and His army!

The Lord also calls the multitudes there by sending three demons ("frogs" from slime pits) to gather them (Rev. 16:13). Nevertheless, there is a great boldness at the cosmic disturbances of the sixth bowl that did not exist at the cosmic disturbances of the sixth seal. Such great destruction will occur that the Israelites, who were "*like the sand by the sea*" will be left with only a remnant (Isa. 10:22). God then promises that His anger will soon end, and that His wrath will be to the destruction of Israel's enemies. But just before that time, He will have one last deed for the Antichrist to do. The course of the Antichrist and his hordes is vividly sketched.

ANTICHRIST'S LAST TREK

"They enter Aiath; they pass through Migron; they store supplies at Micmash. They go over the pass, and say, 'We will camp overnight at Geba.' Ramah trembles; Gibeah of Saul flees. Cry out, O Daughter of Gallim! Listen, O Laishah! Poor Anathoth! Madmenah is in flight; the people of Gebim take cover. This day they will halt at Nob; they will shake their fist at the mount of the Daughter of Zion, at the hill of Jerusalem" (Isa. 10:28-32).

From the book, Thru the Bible With J. Vernon McGee,[46] Dr. McGee comments on the above passages:

"This is a remarkable section of prophecy. It gives geographical locations, all of them north of Jerusalem, and it shows the route taken by Assyria and of the future invader from the north... The invader comes from the land of Magog (see Ezek. 38:39).

"Now notice the places mentioned: 'Aiath' is about fifteen miles north of Jerusalem. 'Migron' is south of Aiath and is the pass where Jonathan got a victory over the Philistines (see 1 Sam. 14). I understand that General Allenby secured a victory over Turkey in the same place. 'Geba' and 'Ramah' are about six miles north of Jerusalem. 'Anathoth' was about three miles north of Jerusalem. This is the home of the prophet Jeremiah. 'Laish' is in the extreme north of Palestine, in the tribe of Dan. 'Madmenah' (dunghill) is a garbage dump north of

---

[46] Vol. 3 p. 225, Thomas Nelson Publishers, Nashville, Tennessee; used with permission.

Jerusalem. 'Gebim' is probably north of Jerusalem. The exact site is not known. 'Nob' is the last place mentioned, and it is north of the city and in sight of Jerusalem.

"This passage clearly charts the march of the enemy from the north, which brings a state of paralysis and defeat to Jerusalem."

The part that was omitted from Dr. McGee's commentary is that he believed this invader from the north to be Russia alone. But Isaiah, in the above chapter, speaks of this day of reckoning to be via the "King of Assyria" (v. 12) with "his thorns and his briars" (v. 17). Many writers and speakers believe that Russia alone is the invader from the North (the "Rosh" of Ezekiel 38:2 and 39:1) and see that battle occurring in the middle or just before the beginning of the tribulation. It is not, as will be shown.

GOG AND MAGOG

The battle of Ezekiel, in chapters 38 and 39, is the end day battle of Armageddon, for it happens, "*On that day...(Ezek. 39:11)*"—*the end day*. The Antichrist (Gog) will be leading Russia and others from the North. There will be types of this battle before the end, perhaps before the seven-year peace covenant with Israel by the Antichrist, referred to in Daniel 9:27. The Antichrist will be in sheep's clothing, and will win a marvelous victory, possibly over Russia, in order to have sufficient "power" to sign the peace covenant. He will appear to many as their deliverer—even their long-awaited Messiah. The Antichrist (like many Bible commentators), will see "Gog" (Ezek. 38:2) as someone other than himself. The Antichrist will then be in a position to claim to be the one who executed the judgement of bloodshed and burning

144

sulfur on the invading troops (Ezek. 38:22)—in essence, claiming to be Israel's deliverer!

───────────── ଔଈଈଔ ─────────────

By placing this battle near the beginning of the Tribulation, it plays right into the hands of the Antichrist and his sponsor, Satan. Think about it. After this battle, the Jews are to live, "in safety in their land with no one to make them afraid" (Ezek. 39:26). They will believe that their long awaited peace has finally arrived.

───────────── ଔଈଈଔ ─────────────

In his book, The Rapture And The Second Coming of Christ,[47] author Finis Dake discusses 12 proofs that this battle in Ezekiel will not be fulfilled in a war between Russia and Israel. He shows 38 predictions in Ezekiel which identify chapters 38 and 39 as being fulfilled at Armageddon. He shows that from the time of the battle and onward, that Israel and other nations know God (38:16; 39:6-7, 21-25, 27); profane his name no more (39:7); that God is glorified by all nations (39:13, 21); and that even the heathen will know what these chapters are about (39:23). Surely, if the heathen—who are without the Holy Spirit to illuminate God's Word—will understand it, then it must be hindsight for them. Hindsight at that time will place the battle at the time of the return of the King of kings.

VALLEY OF JEHOSHAPHAT

We now come to the closing scene. The following morning, the beast prepares to attack Jerusalem. Joel the

───────────────

[47] For ongoing research regarding this battle, the author recommends, "The Rapture And The Second Coming of Christ," by Finis Jennings Dake, Dake Bible Sales, Inc., Lawrenceville, Georgia. The 12 proofs are from chapter five.

prophet foretells the attack: *"Proclaim this among the nations: Prepare for war! Rouse the warriors! Let all the fighting men draw near and attack. Beat your plowshares into swords and your pruning hooks into spears. Let the weakling say, 'I am strong!' Come quickly, all you nations from every side, and assemble there. Bring down your warriors, O Lord! 'Let the nations be roused; let them advance into the Valley of Jehoshaphat, for there I will sit to judge all the nations on every side. Swing the sickle, for the harvest is ripe. Come, trample the grapes, for the winepress is full and the vats overflow; so great is their wickedness!' Multitudes, multitudes in the valley of decision! For the day of the Lord is near in the valley of decision"* (Joel 3:9-14).

The book of Micah gives us the Lord's plan. Many nations will be gathered against Israel, with their intent to defile Zion. *"But they do not know the thoughts of the LORD; they do not understand his plan, he who gathers them like sheaves to the threshing floor"* (Micah 4:12).

The following is taken from the book, The Antichrist, by Arthur W. Pink:[48]

"Once again, though the beast appears to be successful, Jerusalem falls before his onslaught as Jehovah had foretold that it should; *'I will gather all the nations to Jerusalem to fight against it; the city will be captured, the houses ransacked, and the women raped. Half of the city will go into exile, but the rest of the people will not be taken from the city (Zech. 14:2).'* Intoxicated by their success, it is then that the heathen shall rage and the people imagine a vain thing: *'The kings of the earth take their stand and the rulers gather together against the Lord and against his Anointed One. "Let us break their chains," they say, and throw off their fetters'"* (Psalm 2:23).

---

[48] Kregal Publications, Grand Rapids, Michigan, p. 121; used with permission. The NIV version is substituted for the author's KJV version.

MAJOR CITIES TUMBLE DOWN

When all the kings of the world are gathered at Jerusalem, the seventh angel pours out the seventh bowl of his wrath into the air (Rev. 16:17), resulting in the greatest of all earthquakes. Jerusalem splits into three parts, and all other major cities of the world tumble down (Rev. 16:19)—Atlanta, Berlin, Chicago, New York, Miami, Mexico City, Moscow, Paris, Peking, Sao Paulo, San Francisco, Tokyo. Continental land slides, generating great tsunamis (seismic ocean waves) hundreds of feet high and moving at the speed of jet planes, surely will have already inundated most major coastal cities through earlier earthquakes long before this time. Babylon not only tumbles down, but even sinks beneath the earth. Because of the extent of her evil, she is to be utterly destroyed the same as Sodom and Gomorrah (Isa. 13:19; Jer. 50:40). Babylon and all her people are to sink like a stone into the Euphrates River: *"So will Babylon sink to rise no more because of the disaster I will bring upon her. And her people will fall"* (Jer. 51:64).

Jerusalem is the only city to be spared destruction by the mighty earthquake. In this sense, Jerusalem will indeed be like the "Rock of Ages"—Jesus Christ. *"They who trust in the Lord are like Mount Zion, which cannot be shaken but endures forever"* (Psalm 125:1). Jerusalem, and all those who trust in the Lord Jesus, will endure forever!

MOUNTAINS CRUMBLE

Earlier in the tribulation, the mountains and islands had been shaken and moved from their places, but at this immeasurable earthquake, every island fled away and the mountains could not be found. Jerusalem is split into three parts and molten rocks (100 pound hailstones) are cast into the sky (Rev. 16:19-21).

At this point, God will decide that Jerusalem has paid double for all her sins, and that it is time for her to be comforted. The above passage brings us to a voice calling: *"In the desert prepare the way for the Lord; make straight in the wilderness a highway for our God. Every valley shall be raised up, every mountain and hill made low; the rough ground shall become level, the rugged places a plain. And the glory of the Lord will be revealed, and all mankind together will see it. For the mouth of the Lord has spoken"* (Isa. 40:3-5).

"Then the Lord will go out and fight against those nations, as he fights in the day of battle. On that day his feet will stand on the Mount of Olives, east of Jerusalem, and the Mount of Olives will be split in two from east to west, forming a great valley, with half of the mountain moving north and half moving south. You will flee by my mountain valley, for it will extend to Azel. You will flee as you fled from the earthquake in the days of Uzziah king of Judah. Then the Lord my God will come, and all the holy ones with him" (Zech. 14:3-5).

At the revelation of Jesus Christ on the mountain, a pathway for escape will be provided for His chosen people. It will be a protected valley, extending to Azel (which is believed to be about 12 miles east of Jerusalem). But at God's presence, the Gentiles flee out of the city and are scattered, there to join their comrades who are outside of the city for a distance of 1,600 stadia, or 180 miles (Rev. 14:20). This is done in order to spare the future throne at Jerusalem from being defiled with the river of blood that will flow through the land.

FROM MEGIDDO TO BOZRAH

The enemies are gathered as far south as the Edomite stronghold of Bozrah, about twenty miles southeast of the

Dead Sea. The Bible speaks clearly of the Lord coming from Bozrah when His day of vengeance arises. Isaiah 61:2 shows us what will be proclaimed by the Messiah. He will proclaim, *"The year of the Lord's favor and the day of vengeance of our God."* Christ claimed to have fulfilled the day of the Lord's favor when He was here at His first coming.

In Luke 4:18-21, the Messiah stopped reading the Isaiah passage at the word favor, sat down, and informed those there that He had fulfilled the part of the passage that He had read. He fulfills the vengeance part at His second coming, 2,000 years later: *"Who is this coming from Edom, from Bozrah, with his garments stained crimson? Who is this, robed in splendor, striding forward in the greatness of his strength? 'It is I, speaking in righteousness, mighty to save. I have trodden the winepress alone; from the nations no one was with me. I trampled them in my anger and trod them down in my wrath; their blood spattered my garments, and I stained all my clothing. For the day of vengeance was in my heart, and the year of my redemption has come'"* (Isa. 63:1, 3-4).

Not only does Christ vent His anger in Bozrah, but as we'll see in the next chapter, those of us who are in Christ (the believers in Jesus) will join in the Messiah's judgement, after He first sets the example of how to carry out His day of vengeance.

The center of the multitudes is concentrated in the Judean wilderness (opposite Jerusalem) where King Jehoshaphat had a victorious type of this end day battle (2 Chron. 20:20-24). They extend all the way northward through Megiddo, also the scene of an ancient type of this battle (Judges 5:19).

In his book, Revelation Record, Dr. Henry Morris states that if only a small percentage of the future world's population were drafted into an army, it would easily contain more than 200 million soldiers. This would necessitate the soldiers being only five feet apart in order to be within a territory 180 miles wide and a mile deep.

This 180 mile-long stretch will run along what is presently known as the Great Rift, which extends from North Africa to the Sea of Galilee. It will most likely be supported in the north by the port of Haifa, and in the south by the Gulf of Akaba. In this great valley, the river of blood will literally reach to a horse's bridle (Rev. 14:20).

DELIVERER IN ISRAEL

After the Lord's wrath is burned on Jerusalem and Zion, He comes down and fights for her. *"This is what the Lord says to me: 'As a lion growls, a great lion over his prey; and though a whole band of shepherds is called together against him, he is not frightened by their shouts or disturbed by their clamor; so the Lord Almighty will come down to do battle on Mount Zion and on its heights"* (Isa. 31:4).

At this time during the Day of the Lord, He will be against all the people who have been against Israel. He tells them:

"As you have done, it will be done to you; your deeds will return upon your own head...on Mount Zion will be deliverance" (Obad. 15:17).

"And everyone who calls on the name of the Lord will be saved; for on Mount Zion and in Jerusalem there will be deliverance, as the Lord has said, among the survivors whom the Lord calls" (Joel 2:32).

Notice that those Jews who survive and exercise their faith by remaining there in the furnace of judgement, and who will call upon the Lord will be saved. By this time they will all have begged for Christ to rescue them. This deliverance for all of Israel will fulfill the Isaiah 27:9 and 59:20 passages:

"And so all Israel will be saved, as it is written: 'The deliverer will come from Zion; he will turn godlessness away from Jacob. And this is my covenant with them when I take away their sins'" (Rom. 11:26-27).

───────────── ⟨⟩ ─────────────

Some have mistakenly believed that all Israel (or all Jews) are already saved. If that were true, then Christ who came to the lost sheep of the house of Israel was misguided and wasted His death on the cross trying to save people who weren't lost. That is absurd. All of Israel who have not died, will at the end beg for Christ—which is why they will be saved!

───────────── ⟨⟩ ─────────────

BANNER AT JERUSALEM

The deliverer is coming to Zion. *"All you people of the world, you who live on the earth, when a banner is raised on the mountains, you will see it, and when a trumpet sounds, you will hear it"* (Isa. 18:3).

This banner is spoken of in a number of passages. It can mean a banner, ensign, flag, pole, sail, or standard, but generally means a type of signal. In Exodus 17:15, Jehovah is claimed by Moses to be his banner. In the second chapter of Numbers, there was a standard at each point on the compass around the tent of meeting wherein or upon, God located His presence. To the north was the camp of Dan with their standard—an eagle. To the south was the camp of Reuben with their standard—a man. To the east was the camp of Judah with their standard—a lion. And to the west was the camp of Ephraim with their standard—an ox. (The number of people in these four camps form the shape of a cross when viewed from the eastern heavens.) These standards represent what is in heaven; four living creatures surround God's throne. Each, a composite of an eagle, a man, a lion, and an ox.

151

This banner or ensign is associated with God's presence. Isaiah 11:10 states that the root of Jesse (Jesus) shall stand as a banner. This banner is to cause fear and panic.

"'Their stronghold will fall because of terror; at sight of the battle standard their commanders will panic,' declares the Lord, whose fire is in Zion, whose furnace is in Jerusalem" (Isa. 31:9).

"Like birds hovering overhead, the Lord Almighty will shield Jerusalem; he will shield it and deliver it, he will 'pass over' it and will rescue it" (Isa. 31:5).

The picture we have is that the presence of God (the root of Jesse) will be the deliverer. As His banner passes over Jerusalem, the Jews will be rescued.

CLOUD—SIGN OF THE SON OF MAN

In that day, the redeemed of the earth will fly along like clouds, like doves to their nest (Isa. 60:8). This cloud or banner over Israel could be nothing less than the sign (ensign) of the Son of Man. This is clearly spoken of in the Book of Matthew: *"At that time the sign of the Son of Man will appear in the sky, and all the nations of the earth will mourn. They will see the Son of Man coming on the clouds of the sky, with power and great glory"* (Matt. 24:30).

The Antichrist and his hordes are gathered against Jerusalem hoping against hope that Christ and His army (the banner of clouds) will be defeated. The vultures excitedly fly overhead, ready *"for the great supper of God,"* prepared to fulfill prophecy by eating, *"...the flesh of kings, generals, and mighty men,..."* (Rev. 19:17-18). Then Jesus will destroy their leader, the Antichrist, *"...with the breath of his mouth and the splendor of his coming"* (2 Thess. 2:8). The Antichrist will be cast into the Lake of Fire, and his hordes to Hades.

HADES WILL PLAY ITS PART

Hades will be busier than ever. Various beings over time have come and gone, to and from Hades. In the future, most will be going there, but some will be coming out! Hades is the abode for departed spirits. This is where the spirit of Christ went after His crucifixion and before His resurrection, for He *"...descended to the lower, earthly regions"* (Eph. 4:9).

The last sign that the Jews' Messiah was to give to them was the sign of Jonah (Matt. 12:40), that is, that the Son of Man would be three days and nights in the heart of the earth. Many don't realize how close of a sign Jonah was to Christ. Like Christ, Jonah's body was kept in a place, and Jonah (like Christ) was not maintained alive in his tomb (in Jonah's case, the fish), but Jonah literally died and spiritually descended into the pit (Hades): "To the roots of the mountains I sank down; the earth beneath barred me in forever. But you brought my life up from the pit" (Jonah 2:6).

King David knew that a descendant of his would not be abandoned in Sheol (the grave) nor would the body of this Holy One see decay (Acts 2:31). This would fulfill Psalm 16:10 and Christ, of course, did not decay in the tomb! Before Christ's victory on the cross (displayed by His resurrection), the earth had two compartments—one of "comfort" (Paradise) and one of "torment" (Hades). These were separated by "a great gulf" (see Luke 16:23-26). It was here, deep inside the earth, where Christ descended to announce His victory to the spirits imprisoned there (1 Pet. 3:19).

Rebellious *"sons of God"* (fallen angels) during the days of Noah (Gen. 6:2) are in the compartment known in the Greek as Tartarus (2 Pet. 2:4). This is the deepest abyss of Hades—the "gloomy dungeons," according to the New International Version of the Bible. These evil spirits are headed by one named Abaddon—the demon king. They are released from their abyss at the fifth trumpet of Revelation, and apparently in locust-scorpion type bodies (Rev. 9:7).

Another area in Hades is under present day Iraq, under the Euphrates river, where 200 million spirits are located, captained by four fallen angels (Rev, 9:14, 16). Under the torture of the Assyrian (Isa. 8:7) who is actually the Antichrist (as is Shiloah actually Christ as seen in Isa. 8:6), they are released at the sixth trumpet, thirteen months (Rev. 9:15) before the end to promulgate war.

Some of the children of Israel (Isa. 8:18) who curse the King of Israel, their God, are later thrust into utter darkness (Isa. 8:21-22). This dark prison, Hades, is compared to a dungeon (Isa. 24:22), of which it is stated that people will be punished and then released after many days. They will be released to the Lake of Fire to join the damned, 1,000 years later (Rev. 20:14). This is 1,000 years after the Antichrist and the false prophet have been cast there.

Of course, Hades is not only the end destination of some Jews, but for the people of Tyre:

"...then I will bring you down with those who go down to the pit, to the people of long ago. I will make you dwell in the earth below, as in ancient ruins, with those who go down to the pit, and you will not return or take your place in the land of the living" (Eze. 26:20).

Those of Assyria, who are partly composed of the present day people of Iraq, have their end destination in the pit as well: *"They are all destined for death, for the earth below, among mortal men, with those who go down to the* pit" (Eze. 31:14). In Ezekiel 32:18-32, those from Assyria, Edom (Jordan), Egypt, Elam (Iran), Meshech (Russia), Sidon, and Tubal, have their end at the pit.

Satan, who has been such an evil servant of the Lord is to be bound not only in the pit at the end of this present age, but at the bottomless pit, the Abyss (Rev. 20:1).

The Abyss has to be located at the very center of the earth—one could not go down any deeper (because he would then be going up or out) for every boundary is a ceiling. Satan will be as far removed as possible from all human beings (and still be within the earth), and will then remain in the pit, awaiting further use by the Lord 1,000 years later (Rev. 20:3)!

Hades will be busy indeed. All humans, with the exception of Christians, go there at death. There is no such thing as reincarnation, for one dies and is then judged (Heb. 9:27). The Christian believers do not go to Hades, for as shown above, Christ went there in their place. They go straight to Paradise to be "at home with the Lord (2 Cor. 5:8)."

LAKE OF FIRE

The Antichrist king, known also as the Assyrian king, is sent to Topheth, a special place within the Lake of Fire (Isa. 30:33). This is where the most abominable will go. "Topheth" was a place in the valley of Hinnom where the most abominable idolatries were carried out. In this valley in southwest Jerusalem, the Israelites sacrificed their children by burning them in a fire: *"The people of Israel and Judah have provoked me by all the evil they have done; They built high places for Baal in the Valley of Ben Hinnom to sacrifice their sons and daughters to Molech"* (Jer. 32:32, 35).

155

"They have built the high places of Topheth in the Valley of Ben Hinnom to burn their sons and daughters in the fire; something I did not command, nor did it enter my mind" (Jer. 7:31).

It is in this same valley (before the end occurs) that God will repay the Jews for this evil practice, when He fills the valley with the dead of Israel to overflowing; where the birds and beasts will devour (Jer. 7:32, 33).

The Antichrist and his false prophet are to be suddenly snatched from the midst of the people which have invaded Jerusalem and translated at unimaginable speed to the Lake of Fire (Rev. 19:20). The Lake of Fire is not the same place as Sheol or Hades. This is clear from the fact that those who are not saved by accepting Christ's work on the cross (while they were on the earth), are resurrected from Hades (the temporary pit) 1,000 years after the end of our present age, and then cast into the Lake of Fire (Rev. 20:11-15).

Jesus Christ, who is to be the judge of all who have or ever will have lived (John 5:22), spoke of this fiery place on a number of occasions (Matt. 25:41; Mark 9:43-48). These passages have been properly translated as "hell"— the ultimate destination for destruction of those in Hades (located within the earth) when they receive new bodies after the Millennium is over. It is in Gehenna (or the Lake of Fire) where their second death will take place, where both body and soul are destroyed (Matt. 10:28), but where their suffering never ends.

SUMMARY

The end will occur all around the earth. Every eye will see Him, apparently even those who saw Him 2,000 years ago will see Him from hell. The events that lead up to the end are concentrated in the Middle East. It starts at the future rebuilt temple, when the abomination of desolation is set up, which portrays the leader of the future 10-kingdom territory around the Mediterranean Sea. By the end, the wrath and woe will have spread around the world. The earthquake to end all earthquakes occurs worldwide. All major cities tumble to the ground, but Babylon sinks into the earth. Jerusalem is split into three parts, but will be the only city left standing. From the Red Sea, through Jerusalem to the Mediterranean Sea, the enemies of God and the enemies of the Jews will be slain. The Omega returns to the vicinity of Bethany, the area from which He ascended, and physically steps onto the Mt. of Olives. Christ destroys the Antichrist and has him escorted to the Lake of Fire.

CHAPTER 5

WHY DOES IT END?

Back to the Beginning

A question that never seems to be answered sufficiently is, "Why do bad things happen to good people, and good things to bad people?" What people overlook is the fact that paradise was lost at the garden of Eden. God had given dominion to Adam and Eve, but they sinned by disobeying God. In effect, they turned their dominion over to the serpent, the Devil.[49] The good news is that things won't always be in the control of the evil one. The bad news is that things will become even worse before they get better.

We are told in scripture that at the end, at the coming of the Son of Man, everything will be, "*...as it was in the days of Noah*" (Matt. 24:37). Before the Flood, "*The Lord*

---

[49] He is the chief over all who do things their own way, who refuse to submit to God.

saw how great man's wickedness on the earth had become, and that every inclination of the thoughts of his heart was only evil all the time. So the Lord said, `I will wipe mankind, from the face of the earth'" (Gen. 6:5, 7).

"Every living thing on the face of the earth was wiped out" (Gen. 7:23).

As time went by, this catastrophic judgement was deliberately forgotten, and man became bolder in his evil. Even today, people scoff about another impending judgement, exactly as they did before the flood of Noah. It has been stated that everyone has a home somewhere in scripture, and these scoffers certainly have their home in these verses: *"First of all, you must understand that in the last days scoffers will come, scoffing and following their own evil desire. They will say, 'Where is this "coming" he promised? Ever since our forefathers died, everything goes on as it has since the beginning of creation.' But they deliberately forget that long ago by God's word the heavens existed and the earth was formed out of water and by water. By these waters also the world of that time was deluged and destroyed"* (2 Pet. 3:3-6).

GODLESS SCIENCE

If people deliberately ignore the judgement of God on the antediluvians, they are not without "authoritative" support. Unbelieving and atheistic scientists, who are involved in the faith and religion of evolution, misinterpret and misrepresent the fossil evidence, and construct what is known as the geologic column.[50] Through their

---

[50] For further study, the author recommends, "Evolution: The Challenge of the Fossil Record," by Duane Gish, Creation-Life Publishers, Master Books Division, El Cajon, CA, ©1985.

blind faith in this column, which exists nowhere on earth, they construct voluminous ages for the earth. These purported, immeasurable ages allow what they believe is sufficient time for anything to happen; in essence, they believe the old fairy tale that a frog became a prince. (Actually, in all fairness, they believe in the evolution of amoeba to man.) This anti-God (antichrist) theory exists in the mind of man as a purposeful delusion created by the one who currently holds dominion over the earth, the serpent. It deliberately expels God further back in time and space (even if allowed to be present at all) to the point where mens' consciences can feel comfortable, and especially, not answerable to a moral being for their sins.

In order to accomplish his goals, Satan deceived the intellectual and scientific community into re-interpreting God's judgement at the flood of Noah. Thus, with an anti-God thesis as a pre-supposition, an interpretation of a geologic column emerged, removing God completely from the picture. Satan's evolution ministers faithfully preach his religion through every media outlet, and even in educational institutions.

These evolutionists are the progenitors of the scoffers in the above passages. Evolution is not a science that began with Darwin. It is a naturalistic philosophy that tries to explain the existence of all things in terms of natural phenomena and chance happenings. It dates back to the time before Christ's birth.

"Evolutionary ideas began with ancient Greek philosophers such as Epicurus, Aneximendern, Thebes, and Empedocles (2nd to 7th centuries B.C.) not scientists." R. L. Wysong, "The Creation-Evolution Controversy," Inquiry Press, Midland, MI, 1987 (7th printing; 1st in 1976), pg. 44.

Timothy was warned of these evolutionists: *"O Timothy, keep that which is committed to thy trust, avoiding profane [and] vain babbling, and opposition of science falsely so called: Which some professing have erred concerning the faith"* (1 Tim. 6:20-21, KJV).

Certainly one example of "professors of false science" would be those involved in evolutionary scientism. It is this growing godlessness—as it was in the days of Noah—that increasingly ripens the overall state of man for God's wrath and judgement.

Most people realize that there must be an end. If there is a beginning, then there must be an ending. Even science has laws. The First Law of Thermodynamics tells us that matter and energy can neither be created nor destroyed. Since we are here, we must have had a beginning. Thus it also means we had to have had a beginning outside the laws of science-by special creation. The other alternative, evolution, is a vacuous absurdity, totally without substance or credibility. Evolution also depends on a miracle—spontaneous generation—which requires a greater faith for it is not supported by the basic scientific law of cause and effect.

By yet another measure, evolution is more "religious" than creationism. Creationism has given rise to only three religions: Christianity, Judaism, and Islam. Evolution has given rise to the remaining multitude.

Rational thinkers will tell you that things don't run freely uphill. The Second Law of Thermodynamics tells us that things become disordered rather than ordered. Here, evolution directly contradicts one of the most basic laws of science; while creation not only supports, but predicts it. For example, creation tells us that things must have been more uphill in the past, in order to have run so far downhill now. It is this continual "running downhill" that the Creator/Alpha (the Beginning), is going to bring to an end, fulfilling His role as the Consummator/Omega (the End).

We saw in Chapter One, "Who," that the End (Omega) is Jesus Christ, and that He is also the Beginning (Alpha), the Creator. At the end, He will begin to return the earth to the pristine condition in which it was when He created it. It is God's ultimate purpose to bring both the earth and mankind back to a state of perfection, as everything was prior to the time Adam and Eve fell into sin.

END EVIL AND REBELLION

As we see the condition of the world increasingly deteriorating, we shouldn't have to ask why there should be an end. Evil rapidly becomes more and more pervasive, yet people continue to blindly hope for peace and prosperity. For the most part, both the Jews and Gentiles have rejected the Prince of Peace, so they must receive God's coming wrath; only those who are in His will, will escape the wrath (1 Thess. 1:10; 5:9).

God's master plan and purpose through the ages demands that this world system of Satan and man comes to an end. He created both angels and man with a free will. Back at the garden of Eden, it is clear that both fallen angels, 1/3 of the total (Rev. 12:4), and man decided to do their own thing. Immediately, God pronounced judgement and declared that the Eternal Son of God would come to end the rebellion (Gen. 3:15). Since then, the prophecies of the Bible have been many regarding God's plan of salvation, His patient and ongoing dealings with hard-hearted man, and His judgements, past, present, and future. Slowly, the prophecies have been unveiled over time, and many have been fulfilled. It is God's unchanging consistency and the dependable fulfillment of His Word that gives us faith and trust that all remaining prophecy will also be fulfilled.

God has given us prophecy to ensure us that His will, will ultimately be done. In the prayer the Lord taught His disciples, He instructed that they should pray for the kingdom to come, and for God's will to be done on earth, as it is in heaven (Matt. 6:10). Because He said He would, we can believe God will end man's evil and rebellion. Let us look again at His Word for more of the reasons for the coming of the End (the Omega).

JUDGE UNGODLINESS

The end was prophesied by Enoch, the great grand-father of Noah. He also stated the reasons:

"See, the Lord is coming with thousands upon thousands of his holy ones to judge everyone, and to convict all the ungodly of all the ungodly acts they have done in the ungodly way, and of all the harsh words ungodly sinners have spoken against him" (Jude 14-15).

END NON-JEWISH KINGDOMS

The End will come in order to re-establish David's throne and kingdom. The book of Daniel gives us four great empires that would follow David's kingdom—the Babylonian, Medo-Persian, Grecian, and Roman. Revelation 13:2 shows us that these empires will be rebuilt, and together will both endorse the Antichrist and oppose God. The Omega will bring these to an end.

"In the time of those kings, the God of heaven will set up a kingdom that will never be destroyed, nor will it be left to another people. It will crush all those kingdoms and bring them to an end, but it will itself endure forever" (Dan. 2:44).

ESTABLISH CHRIST AS KING OF THE JEWS

At Jesus' crucifixion, the Roman soldiers mocked Him when they put a sign over His head that said, *"King of the Jews."* At the end, all of Christ's mockers will be under the rule of the One whom they unwittingly titled accurately.

"Of the increase of his government and peace there will be no end. He will reign on David's throne and over his kingdom, establishing and upholding it with justice and righteousness from that time on and forever. The zeal of the Lord Almighty will accomplish this" (Isa. 9:7).

Other passages testify to the Kingship of Jesus:

"He will be great and will be called the Son of the Most High. The Lord God will give him the throne of his father David, and he will reign over the house of Jacob forever; his kingdom will never end" (Luke 1:32-33).

Not only will the End rule over Israel, but over all the nations:

"He was given authority, glory and sovereign power; all peoples, nations and men of every language worshiped him. His dominion is an everlasting dominion that will not pass away, and his kingdom is one that will never be destroyed" (Dan. 7:14).

"The Lord will be king over the whole earth" (Zech. 14:9).

The Book of Revelation shows that, in the future, the kingdom of the world will become the Kingdom of the Lord and of His Messiah (Rev. 11:15), and that He will be King of Kings and Lord of Lords (Rev. 19:16).

Some liberal Christians believe that the Church itself is the kingdom, and that by the end the Church will vanquish the kingdoms of the world. In order to believe this, they have to believe that some Christian leader will be over the Islam faiths in places like Iraq or Iran! This idea is unacceptable because Christianity, as man knows it, will never conquer and control the masses. Only God at the end, and at the appointed time, will put an end to all unrighteousness and false religions. Even then, as the King of kings, He will have to rule over them with a rod of iron.

END UNRIGHTEOUSNESS AND INJUSTICE

Righteousness and justice will be established. "The days are coming,' declares the Lord, 'when I will raise up to David a righteous Branch, a King who will reign wisely and do what is just and right in the land'" (Jer. 23:5).

God warns the world that at the end He will judge the world because of the injustice that went on during man's "week"—that He has not forgotten the sins of mankind. Justice demands that sin be judged.

"'In that day,' declares the Sovereign Lord, 'the songs in the temple will turn to wailing. Many, many bodies; flung everywhere! Silence!' Hear this, you who trample the needy and do away with the poor of the land...skimping the measure, boosting the price and cheating with dishonest scales... 'I will never forget anything they have done.' Will not the land tremble, for this, and all who live in it mourn" (Amos 8:3-5, 8)?

END OLD KINGS AND ESTABLISH NEW KINGS

One reason why the ways of this world will end should be of real interest to the saints of God, who, as far as economic, political, and social power, have been closer to the tail than the head. The Lord will "impeach" those in power and give the rule over all societal and material things to His saints.

"But the saints of the Most High will receive the kingdom and will possess it forever; yes, for ever and ever. As I watched, the **horn** *was waging war against the saints and defeating them until the Ancient of Days came and pronounced judgment in favor of the saints of the Most High, and the time came when they possessed the kingdom. Then the sovereignty, power and greatness of the kingdoms under the whole heaven will be handed over to the saints, the people of the Most High"* (Dan. 7:18, 22, 27).

The sixth chapter of 1 Corinthians speaks of the identity of the above mentioned saints, after clearly telling us who they are not. It is elaborated there that they are not the homosexuals, thieves, drunkards, prostitutes, and adulterers. Rather, they are those who are washed and sanctified, who are justified in the name of the Lord Jesus Christ and by the Spirit of God.

The Omega ends the ways of this world, in order to turn things over to His saints, those who have accepted God's provision (or sacrifice) for their sins—the Omega Himself.

The horn mentioned above in Daniel 7 is the future (and last) mighty king, the Antichrist. He, along with his priest, the false prophet, have the distinguished "honor" of being the first two individuals to be thrown into the Lake of Fire (Rev. 19:20). This is an especially significant reason why the Lord will return—to bring these two to an end.

REGATHER ISRAEL AND BUILD THE TEMPLE

As stated in the following scriptures, the Messiah will come and regather all Israel and build His Millennial Temple.

"He will raise a banner for the nations and gather the exiles of Israel; he will assemble the scattered people of Judah from the four quarters of the earth" (Isa. 11:12).

"At that time the sign of the Son of Man will appear in the sky, and all the nations of the earth will mourn. They will see the Son of Man coming on the clouds of the sky, with power and great glory. And he will send his angels with a loud trumpet call, and they will gather his elect from the four winds, from one end of the heavens to the other" (Matt. 24:30-31).

He comes not only to regather the Israelites, but to build the temple and to be clothed with majesty, where He will be a priest on the throne (Zech. 6:13). He will reveal His glory (Isa. 40:5), so that from that day forward the house of Israel will know that He is the Lord their God (Ezek. 39:22).

SEPARATE THE SHEEP AND GOATS

"When the Son of Man comes in his glory, and all the angels with him, he will sit on his throne in heavenly glory. All the nations will be gathered before him, and he will separate the people one from another as a shepherd separates the sheep from the goats" (Matt. 25:31-32).

According to Matthew 24:15-20, the sheep will be gathered from the people of the obedient ones who, for example, will have fled to the hills for refuge. They will also be composed of those who did good works; those who gave supplies of food, water, clothing, and visited those who were sick or in prison. They will enter the Millennial Kingdom and continue with extended life, bearing children under near perfect conditions.

The goats will be those habitual sinners who didn't have the good works, and who will hear those awful words, *"Depart from me, you who are cursed, into the eternal fire prepared for the devil and his angels"* (Matt. 25:41).

In Matthew 24:38-39, these goats are compared to those who did not choose the ark in Noah's day and were taken away by the flood. Verse 39 clearly states that they will likewise be taken away:

"For in the days before the flood, people were eating and drinking, marrying and giving in marriage, up to the day Noah entered the ark; and they knew nothing about what would happen until the flood came and took them all away. That is how it will be at the coming of the Son of Man."

Christ describes the judgement over which He will preside in His own words, and refers to the goats as weeds:

"As the weeds are pulled up and burned in the fire, so it will be at the end of the age. The Son of Man will send out his angels, and they will weed out of his kingdom everything that causes sin and all who do evil" (Matt. 13:40-41).

END RELIGION

The End will come to do away with religion. Religion gives someone a work to do, so that he can be "accepted" of God. But what God desires is a relationship, and the only "work" involved is simple acceptance—all the necessary work has already been done at the cross!

Religion has its roots in Babylon. It is *"THE MOTHER OF PROSTITUTES AND OF THE ABOMINATIONS OF THE EARTH"* (Rev. 17:5). [51] The so called "New Age" religion of today is the same religion that was at Babylon. A god of any description is acceptable; people are trying again to reach fulfillment under their own power and

---

[51] Capitalization is from scripture.

direction, as it was in the days of ancient Babylon: *"Then they said, 'Come, let us build ourselves a city, with a tower that reaches to the heavens, so that we may make a name for ourselves and not be scattered over the face of the whole earth'"* (Gen. 11:4).

All apostate religions[52] are summed up in this Mystery Babylon, which will have so much political clout that even the beast (the Antichrist) will be ridden by her for a time (Rev. 17:3).

END THE JEWS' REBELLION

The End will come because of the sin and rebellion of the Jews. The Bible asks the question, "Why?" for the Jews, and then provides the answer.

"'Why has the Lord done such a thing to this land and to this temple?' People will answer, 'Because they have forsaken the Lord, the God of their fathers, who brought them out of Egypt, and have embraced other gods, worshiping and serving them; that is why he brought all this disaster on them'" (2 Chron. 7:21-22).

The Lord will fulfill the promises of curses for Israel's rebellion against Him: *"All Israel has transgressed your law and turned away, refusing to obey you. 'Therefore the curses and sworn judgments written in the Law of Moses, the servant of God, have been poured out on us, because we have sinned against you'"* (Dan. 9:11). This is to happen because of the sins of Israel's leaders, *"...who shed within her the blood of the righteous"* (Lam. 4:13).

They will ask this, even though they are given the

---

[52] The classic definition is a political defection; referring to Christianity it is a conscious religious defection, a secession from the Church, and a disowning of the name of Christ.

answer quite succinctly (and in an historic nutshell) by the first martyr of Christ the Messiah—Stephen, in the 7th chapter of Acts.

SPRINKLE THOSE WHO CRUCIFIED CHRIST

Jeremiah is a type of the Messiah who compares himself to a lamb. He had been a gentle "lamb" who was led to the slaughter. They wanted to, *"...cut him off from the land of the living"* (Jer. 11:19). This passage is clearly the type of the man of sorrows (Jesus Christ) described in Isaiah 53: *"...he was led like a lamb to the slaughter. For he was cut off from the land of the living"* (Isa 53:7-8).

At the crucifixion of the Messiah, *"All the people answered, 'Let his blood be on us and on our children'"* (Matt. 27:25)! At the cross, His appearance was disfigured and, *"...marred beyond human likeness, so he will sprinkle [shed the blood of] many"* (Isa. 52:14-15).

Because the Messiah's people have rejected Him, *"the gentle flowing waters of Shiloh,"* He will bring, *"the king of Assyria"* (the Antichrist) to overrun and overflow His people (Isa. 8:6-7). Since all have sinned and fallen short of the glory of God, and not just His own people (Rom. 3:23), the Lord will also shed the blood of Gentiles who have rejected Him (Rev. 14:18).

The Bible makes it very clear that all people are responsible for crucifying Christ, even though the plan of salvation was God's plan and will. *"Indeed Herod and Pontius Pilate met together with the Gentiles and the people of Israel in this city to conspire against your holy servant Jesus, whom you anointed. They did what your power and will had decided beforehand should happen"* (Acts 4:27-28).

The wages of sin is death (Rom. 6:23). But the good news is that since God's Son had no sin, then His death opens the way to life for all who believe in Him as their sacrifice.

END VIOLENCE, EVIL GAIN, & GENTILE RULE

God will put an end once again to the violence on the earth, just as He did in the days of Noah (Gen. 6:1). He will come to end the prosperity of the wicked (Jer. 12:1), and the times of the Gentiles (Luke 21:24), who have ruled over Israel since 606 B.C.

END THE CURSE

Many prophecies and promises of God show with abundant clarity that at the end the Omega will consummate the curse on the world. Here are a few:

"The creation waits in eager expectation for the sons of God to be revealed. For the creation was subjected to frustration, not by its own choice, but by the will of the one who subjected it, in hope that the creation itself will be liberated from its bondage to decay and brought into the glorious freedom of the children of God" (Rom. 8:19-21).

"...no longer will there be any curse" (Rev. 22:3).

"The desert and the parched land will be glad; the wilderness will rejoice and blossom. The burning sand will become a pool, the thirsty ground bubbling springs. In the haunts where jackals once lay, grass and reeds and papyrus will grow" (Isa. 35:1, 7).

"They will come and shout for joy on the heights of Zion; they will rejoice in the bounty of the Lord; the grain, the new wine and the oil, the young of the flocks and herds. They will be like a well-watered garden, and they will sorrow no more" (Jer. 31:12).

"No longer will there be any curse" (Rev. 22:3).

END PAIN, SICKNESS, & PREMATURE DEATH

For those of us who have practiced in the healing arts and sciences there is great news. At the end, dentists, nurses, physicians, etc., will suddenly become underemployed or unemployed!

"There will be no more death or mourning or crying or pain, for the old order of things has passed away" (Rev. 21:4).

"Then will the eyes of the blind be opened and the ears of the deaf unstopped. Then will the lame leap like a deer, and the mute tongue shout for Joy" (Isa. 35:5-6).

"Never again will there be in it an infant that lives but a few days, or an old man who does not live out his years; he who dies at a hundred will be thought a mere youth" (Isa. 65:20).

END WARS AND WRONG POSSESSION

"He will judge between many peoples and will settle disputes for strong nations far and wide. They will beat their swords into plowshares and their spears into pruning hooks. Nation will not take up sword against nation, nor will they train for war anymore" (Micah 4:3).

God will end the wrong possession of the earth. In the beginning, God gave rule and dominion to Adam (Gen. 1), who in turn gave it to Satan at the Fall (Gen. 2). God promised to reclaim it through the Messiah (Gen. 3), Who is the second and last Adam (Rom. 5:14).

Christ is the Kinsman, the Redeemer of mankind. He paid the price for redemption by shedding His blood (Rev. 5:9). At the end, He will evict Satan and his forces from their temporary position of authority on the earth (Rev. 19:20; 20:3). He then establishes the theocratic rule as it was intended for Adam, the first man (and the last until Christ), who was created in His image.

"I have installed my King on Zion, my holy hill. Ask of me, and I will make the nations your inheritance, the ends of the earth your possession" (Psalms 2:6, 8).

END UNJUST GOVERNMENT

Among the many other ends that humanity will welcome with open arms will be the end to unjust politics and political systems, including tyrants and dictators.

"For to us a child is born [Son of Man—testifying to his humanity], *to us a son is given* [Son of God—testifying to his divinity],... *And he will be called Wonderful Counselor, Mighty God, Everlasting Father, Prince of Peace. Of the increase of his government and peace there will be no end. He will reign on David's throne and over his kingdom, establishing and upholding it with justice and righteousness from that time on and forever"* (Isa. 9:6-7).

"He was given authority, glory and sovereign power; all peoples, nations and men of every language worshiped him. His dominion is an everlasting dominion that will not pass away, and his kingdom is one that will never be destroyed" (Dan. 7:14).

END APATHY TOWARDS JERUSALEM

Throughout recorded history, the Jewish nation has been the recipient of unjust prejudice and persecution. This, too, will end.

"At that time they will call Jerusalem The Throne of the Lord, and all nations will gather in Jerusalem to honor the name of the Lord. No longer will they follow the stubbornness of their evil hearts" (Jer. 3:17).

"On that day living water will flow out from Jerusalem, half to the eastern sea and half to the western sea, in summer and in winter. The Lord will be king over the whole earth" (Zech. 14:8-9).

END TEARS AND SORROW

God will end the tears and sorrow of the Jews. *"They will enter Zion with singing; everlasting joy will crown their heads. Gladness and joy will overtake them, and sorrow and sighing will flee away"* (Isa. 35:10). Their days of sorrow will end (Isa. 60:20). They will receive, *"...a garment of praise instead of a spirit of despair"* (Isa. 6:13), and, *"...comfort and joy instead of sorrow"* (Jer. 31:13).

To the rest of the multitudes, from every nation, tribe, people and language—to whoever becomes an inheritance of God's during the tribulation, God gives this great promise, *"And God will wipe away every tear from their eyes"* (Rev. 7:17).

SUMMARY

After Israel has been purified in the furnace of the tribulation, she will be ready for repentance (turning to God). He will have judged her for her sins, including the rejection of Himself as Messiah. He will end the Gentile domination over Israel, and convert the entire nation of Israel in that one day (Zech. 3:9; Isa. 66:8). What a glorious future is in store for Israel and the Jewish people!

The tribulation (the time of Jacob's trouble) is not only for the Jews who have rejected God, but for all the sons of Adam (mankind in general). From the garden of Eden onward, man has elected to do his own thing. There will be nothing left for the Creator to do but to bring it all to an end. He is coming to punish man for his sin (Isa. 26:21) and to judge and avenge for bloodshed (Rev. 6:10). He is coming to crush some (Psalm 110:6) and to rule others with an iron rod (Psalm 2:9). Through the ages, He will have shown the world that man without God can only create havoc and heartache, that sinful mankind, left long enough to himself, will not find his own fulfillment under his own power, but rather will only destroy himself, the earth, and everything in it (Matt. 24:22; Rev. 11:18).

The Omega comes to end the ungodly systems of today. He has shown grace to the wicked, but the wicked continue in their evil and rebellion (Isa. 26:10). The Judge will judge man and punish him for the blood that he has shed and the sins he has committed (Rev 6:10, 26:21); He will reward everyone according to what they have done.

CHAPTER 6

HOW DOES IT END?

Scriptures Give Details

"How" questions always seem to be the most intriguing. Certainly the question, "How does it end?" is no exception. We are given many details about the end of the world within the pages of the Bible, more than what many may believe. As we have seen, there are a considerable number of prophecies throughout God's Word relating to this last day of man and the beginning of the 1,000-year Day of the Lord. Many more relate to how it ends.

As we saw in Chapter Three, "WHEN," the end will take place on Tishri 10, on the festival of Yom Kippur, which is the highest holy day of the year for Jews. All faithful Israelites who are left after their purification through the tribulation, will on that day petition God with prayer.

Earlier, we saw where God said He was going back to His place to hide until in their misery the Israelites would seek His face (Hos. 5:15). They will ask, *"Why do you hide your face and forget our misery and oppression"* (Psalm 44:24)?

REVEALED IN MIGHT

The petition of the Jews at the end will be: *"Do not hide your face from me... Let the morning bring me word of your unfailing love, for I have put my trust in you"* (Psalm 143:7-8).

After praising God, they will add: *"Part your heavens, O Lord, and come down; touch the mountains, so that they smoke. Send forth lightning and scatter* [the enemies]; *shoot your arrows and rout them"* (Psalm 144:5-6).

In 2 Samuel 22, and identical verses in Psalm 18, King David is shown as a type of future Israel. After the Jews offer the above prayer, we see God answering it. Below, the Word of God gives us the details:

"In my distress I called to the Lord; I called out to my God. From his temple he heard my voice; my cry came to his ears. The earth trembled and quaked, the foundations of the heavens shook; they trembled because he was angry. Smoke rose from his nostrils; consuming fire came from his mouth, burning coals blazed out of it. He parted the heavens and came down; dark clouds were under his feet. He mounted the cherubim and flew; he soared on the wings of the wind. He made darkness his canopy around him; the dark rain clouds of the sky.

*"He reached down from on high and took hold of me; he drew me out of deep waters. He rescued me from my powerful enemy, from my foes, who were too strong for me. They confronted me in the **day of my disaster**, but the Lord was my support"* (2 Sam. 22:7-12, 17-19).

We see at the close of the above passage that the setting for this is, "in the day of my disaster"—the day of the

Lord. This will be the end day, and the end for Israel's enemies. We see that at the Jews request to, "...part your heavens, O Lord, and come down," that indeed, "...he parted the heavens and came down"!

EARTH TREMBLES

As the Lord approaches the earth, it begins to tremble:
"The mountains quake before him and the hills melt away. The earth trembles at his presence, the world and all who live in it" (Nah. 1:5).

"The earth is broken up, the earth is split asunder, the earth is thoroughly shaken. The earth reels like a drunkard, it sways like a hut in the wind; so heavy upon it is the guilt of its rebellion that it falls; never to rise again" (Isa. 24:19-20).

Apparently, the earth begins to literally "rock and roll." Before the earth begins to shake, the nations begin to tremble, the mountains crumble (Hab. 3:6), and God comes from a place called Teman,[53] a city in Edom (named after the descendents of Esau, at the southeast border of Palestine; see footnote). In Isaiah 63:1-6, we are told that the One coming from Edom comes in splendor, His garments stained with blood. This one is the Lord, who is coming in person against Israel's enemies on His day of vengeance.

BUZZARDS GATHER

The vultures will darken the sky as they circle overhead (Rev. 19:17), surely filling the armies gathered

---

[53] The chief stronghold of Edom; Edomites had once been celebrated for their courage and wisdom (Jer. 49:7), but were doomed in a prophecy by Ezekiel (25:13).

against Israel with fear and dread. For this is the sacrifice that the Lord has prepared, and the vultures will be part of His "guests" (Zeph. 1:7). The Lord will cause the enemies of Israel to stumble like blind men before He pours out their blood and entrails (Zeph 1:17). The bloodshed is massive and sudden, so much so that it can only be described as grapes being trampled.

DAY OF DARKNESS

Most people associate the Lord with light, as it should be. But when He comes as a judge, He will be accompanied by darkness.

"Will not the day of the Lord be darkness, not light— pitch dark, without a ray of brightness" (Amos 5:20)?

"Clouds and thick darkness surround him" (Psalm 97:2).

GOD'S THUNDERING VOICE

Before Omega steps onto the Mount of Olives, His voice comes from the temple in heaven (Rev. 17:17). The reverberating majestic voice will be none other than God's. This voice is the same voice that cried out, "in a loud voice" 2,000 years earlier. There He had just completed His work of redemption, and from the cross cried, *"It is finished"* (John 19:30).

Now in His glory, Christ appears to have a much stronger voice! For after the seventh bowl judgement hits the atmosphere of the earth, the voice from the throne in heaven shouts, *"It is done"* (Rev. 16:17)! Omega utters these conclusive words from heaven, just before returning to earth.

At that time, the Lord will have no need to wait any longer before returning. At Calvary, He placed the judgement on Himself. Over the centuries, especially through the tribulation, He poured out ever increasing judgement; ever pointing sinners to His cross for salvation and escape. All that is left now is to return and physically remove the wicked from the earth.

"See, the Name of the Lord comes from afar, with burning anger and dense clouds of smoke; his lips are full of wrath, and his tongue is a consuming fire. And you will sing as on the night you celebrate a holy festival... The Lord will cause men to hear his majestic voice and will make them see his arm coming down with raging anger and consuming fire, with cloudburst, thunderstorm and hail. Topheth has long been prepared; it has been made ready for the king. Its fire pit has been made deep and wide, with an abundance of fire and wood; the breath of the Lord, like a stream of burning sulfur, sets it ablaze" (Isa. 30:27, 29-30, 33).

(Readers will note that the above passage suggests the event taking place on a holy festival day.)

JUDGEMENTS REMODEL EARTH

It is after Omega's great shout that earth experiences the incomparably worst earthquake of all time. Since this seventh bowl is poured onto the surrounding atmosphere, all the earth is sentenced to the quake. The Old Testament prophets specifically foresaw this judgement:

"In my zeal and fiery wrath I declare that at that time there shall be a great earthquake in the land of Israel" (Ezek. 38:19).

"I will shake all nations, and the desired of all nations will come..." (Haggai 2:7).

It is this final, worldwide earthquake that will change the entire earth's topography. As mountain ranges all over the world sink, all the chief cities around the world will come tumbling down. Only Jerusalem will endure!

"Those who trust in the Lord are like Mount Zion, which cannot be shaken but endures forever" (Psalm 125:1).

Through this cataclysm, God will make things beautiful for the Millennium. Zion is to be beautiful and lofty (Psalm 48:2). After the polluted cities are leveled, new, peaceful cities will be erected. The earthquake will eliminate the great mountain ranges and islands of the world. God will restore the gentle, more level topography that was present before the last great cataclysm of Noah's Flood.

"Every valley shall be raised up, every mountain and hill made low; the rough ground shall become level, the rugged places a plain" (Isa. 40:4).

Because of the tribulation period, the heavenly bodies splashing down, worldwide drought, and the intensified solar radiation, much of the water vapor canopy will be restored. This will restore the tropical climates that the dinosaurs and Noah enjoyed before the Flood. This global greenhouse will again support abundant plant growth, and prevent mass movements of air such as hurricanes and tornadoes. Cool underwater subterranean springs will also be formed (Isa. 41:18).

Surely the volcanic upheavals and the atmospheric bombardments will resupply the soil with nutrients and trace elements. The innumerable dead plants, animals, and yes, people, will (like Jezebel) become fertilizing agents, adding organic nutrients to the soils as well. Death will then yield life.

LIGHTNING, THUNDERSTORMS, & TIDAL WAVES

"The nations were angry; and your wrath has come. The time has come for judging the dead, and for rewarding your servants the prophets and your saints and those who reverence

your name, both small and great; and for destroying those who destroy the earth. Then God's temple in heaven was opened, and within his temple was seen the ark of his covenant. And there came flashes of lightning, rumblings, peals of thunder, an earthquake and a great hailstorm" (Rev. 11:18-19).

The Psalms give us a description of how the revelation of the Omega will occur: *"Out of the brightness of his presence clouds advanced, with hailstones and bolts of lightning. The Lord thundered from heaven; the voice of the Most High resounded. He shot his arrows and scattered [the enemies], great bolts of lightning and routed them. The valleys of the sea were exposed and the foundations of the earth laid bare at your rebuke, O Lord, at the blast of breath from your nostrils"* (Psalm 18:12-15).

The book of Habakkuk expounds on the above passage: *"Rays will flash from his hand where his power is hidden"* (Hab 3:4). As the mountains sink, the deep (the sea) roars and lifts its waves, sending torrents of water (Hab 3:10). Great tidal waves will sweep across the land, as it rises and sinks (Amos 9:5). This, along with the earth changing its axial orientation[54] (Isa. 24:20) will cause extensive flooding of coastlines and beyond.

ANGELIC CLOUDS

We have seen that the coming of the Son of Man will be accompanied with clouds; indeed it is assured by Christ's own words (Matt. 24:30). He will mount the cherubim (the angels surrounding His throne) and come down. The cherubim/chariot (an immense cloud) is described in the first chapter of Ezekiel. God has a number of other chariots as well:

---

[54] Perhaps to prepare continuous sunlight at the earth's poles.

"*The chariots of God are tens of thousands and thousands of thousands*" (Psalm 68:17). We are reminded by Enoch that, "*...the Lord is coming with thousands upon thousands of his holy ones to judge everyone*" (Jude 14). Clouds, chariots, and angels are all closely associated (Psalm 104:3-4).

When the Lord is revealed from heaven, it will be with chariots and blazing fire (Isa. 66:15), and with angels and flaming fire (2 Thess. 1:2). At the end, He will be with all His saints (1 Thess. 3:13). What a glorious procession it will be! Those of us who have been redeemed by Christ, along with the angels, will come back to the earth!

THE SAINTS GO MARCHING OUT

The saints will march out to execute judgement! "*Let the saints rejoice in this honor and sing for joy on their beds. May the praise of God be in their mouths and a double-edged sword in their hands, to inflict vengeance on the nations and punishment on the peoples, to bind their kings with fetters, their nobles with shackles of iron, to carry out the sentence written against them. This is the glory of all his saints*" (Psalm 149:5-9).

After the long "week" is finally over, during which the god of this age (the Devil) ruling with his principals, powers, evil spirits (Eph. 6:12), and Christ-rejecting human deceivers—it all ends. Moreover, God's angels and those of us who are in Christ will become executioners. We will then be like the angels in the spirit realm.

Angels have carried out God's battles in the past, but this time, those who are in Christ, who will have been removed from the earth by death or rapture (taken away from the earth while alive, like Elijah), will act in concert with the angels. We will perform supernatural things.

Once God wills that supernatural beings are to be

employed, the last day battle of Armageddon will be brief, but climactic. The Messiah of Israel has informed all that, at His request, He can muster more than twelve legions of angels (Matt. 26:53), which He will do on this final day battle. He will thus have more than sufficient "fire power." However, since even in his glory, man's frame is from the dust, this end battle of good over evil will be over as soon as it starts.

HISTORICAL TYPES TO BE FULFILLED

Historical events and persons in the Old Testament are symbolic of things in the New Testament, even things that will occur years or millennia later. As previously shown, this is known as a "type" or "prototype." For example, Abraham offering Isaac is a "type" of God the Father offering God the Son.

The prophet Zechariah spoke of men, *"...who are men symbolic of things to come"* (Zech. 3:8). The prophet Isaiah spoke of people who, *"...are signs and symbols in Israel"* (Isa. 8:18). The Apostle Paul informs us, *"These things happened to them as examples and were written down as warnings for us, on whom the fulfillment of the ages has come"* (1 Cor. 10:11).

Therefore, once again history will repeat itself, at least in type, at the Battle of Armageddon. Furthermore, the Valley of Jehoshaphat (known today as the Kidron Valley) is the same valley in which the end-time battle will take place (Joel 3:2; 3:12).

Inflicting Madness

The armies attempting to march against Jerusalem will be struck with madness (Zech. 12:4). In the past, God sent a panic along with an earthquake (1 Sam. 14:15), and confused an opposing army, to the point that they began to strike each other with their weapons (1 Sam. 14:20). The ancient battles of Israel clearly show that Sovereign God has intervened with supernatural elements, and we can be assured that He will not hesitate to employ the same methods again.

Sun Goes Out

The Amorite Kings of long ago were thrown into confusion when hailstones came out of the sky; and something supernatural happened to the sun (Josh. 10:10-13). At the end, we see the fulfillment of this type. God will use hailstones once again (Rev. 16:21), and the sun will be supernaturally controlled at noon (Amos 8:9).

Confusion and Terror

God has thrown the enemies of Israel into confusion on a number of occasions. Gideon defeated the Midianites when the Lord caused them to turn on each other with their swords at the time Gideon's men blew their trumpets (Judges 7:22). God again confused Israel's enemies at the time of Jehoshaphat. The Israelites were so out numbered that singing praises and petitioning the Lord were all they could do. The Lord answered their prayer and confused the enemies so that they killed one another (2 Chron. 20:23). We saw earlier that the Angel of the Lord, the End or Omega (Jesus) put to death a hundred and eighty-five thousand in one night, before the sun rose (2 Kings 19:35). Also, God struck terror into the Arameans and caused them to flee at twilight when they heard the supernatural sound of chariots, and a great army (2 Kings 7:6-7).

Supernatural Beings Will Battle

Heavenly beings have long been employed by God in His armed forces. On one occasion, King David was able to hear God's supernatural army that was to go out ahead of Him to fight the battle.

"As soon as you hear the sound of marching in the tops of the balsam trees, move quickly, because that will mean the Lord has gone out in front of you to strike the Philistine army" (2 Sam. 5:24).

After a prayer by Elisha, a servant was able to actually see the Lord's supernatural army. *"And Elisha prayed, 'O Lord, open his eyes so he may see.' Then the Lord opened the servant's eyes, and he looked and saw the hills full of horses and chariots of fire all around Elisha"* (2 Kings 6:17). The invading enemy forces were later struck with blindness.

These Old Testament battles were all "types." All of the supernatural elements of these ancient battles of Israel will again be used in the brief battle at Armageddon, as shown later. As her judge, the Lord is terrible and fearful to Israel; as her defender, He is even more fearful!

After the Antichrist and his forces have gone into Jerusalem and are ransacking houses and raping women (Zech. 14:2), the Lord decides to fight for Israel as in days gone by!

"The Lord God will come, and all the holy ones with him" (Zech. 14:5).

"Like dawn spreading across the mountains, a large and mighty army comes, such as never was of old nor ever will be again. Before them fire devours; behind them a flame blazes" (Joel 2:2-3).

"The Lord thunders at the head of his army; his forces are beyond number..." (Joel 2:11).

We who are in Christ (either by death or rapture) are

in this formidable army. We will meet the army described in Isaiah 5:26 that, by earth's standards, is certainly formidable. This earthly army will be the same army God will have used to purify/refine His chosen people, where the bodies of the Jews will be, *"...like refuse in the streets"* (Isa. 5:25).

A BANNER OVER JERUSALEM

A banner will attract the anti-Christian armies to Jerusalem (Isa. 5:26). At the same time, the Messianic Christian army from heaven comes (Isa. 13:3-5). This banner has to have a balance to it. It has to look powerful enough to attract all of the world's armies, but not so powerful as to make them flee prematurely. Certainly all the armies of the world will not be needed to finish crushing the few remaining Jews in Israel. Perhaps the banner will be the 144,000, sealed supernaturally from physical harm, for they are seen at the end on Mount Zion with the Lamb, the Messiah of Israel (Rev. 14:1). On the other hand, it's hard to believe that if the Messiah of Israel (Who is God Himself) is there, that any army or armies would be foolish enough to come against Him with any number in their ranks or sophistication of weaponry! Perhaps Christ will at first be unrevealed of His eminent glory by the surrounding darkness (Psalm 97:2) in order to permit the Antichrist's armies to gather up for their impending annihilation.

In the Old Testament, a thousand Israelites had fled from the threat of one (Isa. 30:17). Soon it will be time to reverse the role. As in the days of Joshua, a thousand of the enemy will be routed by one Israeli (Josh. 23:10). Once the Jews realize that their Messiah will have arrived to fight for them, they will acquire a boldness beyond description:

"On that day the Lord will shield those who live in Jerusalem, so that the feeblest among them will be like David, and the house of David will be like God, like the Angel of the Lord going before them" (Zech. 12:8).

God has set precedents in the way He acts on the earth. Once the Israelites see that the Holy One is with them, they will boldly move out. Just as David waited until he heard the marching of the troops in the tops of the balsam trees, and then moved quickly (2 Sam. 5:24), the Israelites will do the same. When they hear and perceive the supernatural army, who will then be in the spiritual realm over Jerusalem, and know that we are ready to fight for them, they will move out fearlessly! In order for the battle to be over as quickly as it is foretold, it is possible that the Jews there will only have to do so much as point a finger at someone, and we (the heavenly Army of Christ) will slay them.

Great Ball of Fire

"The Light of Israel will become a fire, their Holy One a flame; in a single day it will burn and consume his thorns and his briers" (Isa. 10:17).

The Holy One is the coming Messiah of Israel. Since Romans tells us that none is righteous and that all have sinned (3:10, 23), it shows that in accordance with Isaiah 9:6, this Holy One is the God-Man. There is only One Whom it could be—the Lion from the tribe of Judah, their true Messiah, Who returns to fight for His beloved Israel.

The Messiah personally takes care of His worn-out servant, the Antichrist. This false messiah, along with Satan, has enjoyed great earthly "success"—particularly against the Jews. However, that success will have come to an end as the Messiah is to destroy him, *"…by the splendor of his coming"* (2 Thess. 2:8). With such unveiled splendor, no one on earth will doubt that it is God Almighty, King of the Jews, who has come to claim the ultimate victory.

"God came from Teman, the Holy One from Mount Paran. His glory covered the heavens and his praise filled the earth. His splendor was like the sunrise; rays flashed from his hand, where his power was hidden" (Hab. 3:3-4).

The beast (Antichrist), the kings of the earth, and their armies will be gathered together to make war against the King of kings and Lord of lords (Rev. 19:19). The beast (their leader) will be snatched up and swiftly escorted alive to Gehenna, the lake of fire (Rev. 19:20, 20:10, 14, 15). In addition to having been a place of idolatrous sacrifice,[55] Gehenna served in Jesus' time as a receptacle of refuse outside of Jerusalem. Jesus used its perpetually burning fires as illustrations of the coming judgements. Gehenna is not to be confused with Hades, an intermediary place of the wicked. (For a more detailed discussion, see the sections, "Hades Will Play Its Part" and "Lake of Fire" in Chapter Four.) The name is derived from Ben Hinnom, a valley in Israel. An area in the valley of Hinnom was Topheth, and its association with the Antichrist king is made clear:

"Topheth has long been prepared; it has been made ready for the king. Its fire pit has been made deep and wide, with an abundance of fire and wood; the breath of the Lord, like a stream of burning sulfur, sets it ablaze" (Isa. 30:33).

It is at this time that fire will come down from heaven and devour the world's army (Ps. 97:3; Rev. 20:9), fulfilling a promise in Hebrews 10:27, *"...a fearful expectation of judgement and of raging fire that will consume the enemies of God."*

---

[55] Gehenna is the place where the Jews offered their children to Molech, by burning them in the fire (2 Kings 23:10; Jer. 7:31; 19:2-6).

JEWS ARISE FOR VICTORY

"The house of Jacob will be a fire and the house of Joseph a flame" (Obad. 1:18).

"Then the leaders of Judah will say in their hearts, 'The people of Jerusalem are strong, because the Lord Almighty is their God.' On that day I will make the leaders of Judah like a firepot in a woodpile, like a flaming torch among sheaves. They will consume right and left all the surrounding peoples, but Jerusalem will remain intact in her place" (Zech. 12:5-6).

Some are burnt on the tops of their heads (Jer. 48:45). Others will be seized with terror: *"They will writhe like a woman in labor. They will look aghast at each other, their faces aflame"* (Isa. 13:8).

"The peoples will be burned as if to lime; like cut thornbushes they will be set ablaze" (Isa. 33:12).

INSTANTANEOUS NECROSIS

The Lord also describes what is more than just fire. *"Therefore, the Lord, the LORD Almighty, will send a **wasting disease** upon his [Antichrist's] sturdy warriors; under his pomp a fire will be kindled like a blazing flame"* (Isa. 10:16).

Here the Lord associates a wasting disease with fire, but this fire is, "like a blazing flame." A fire is something that releases complex matters like hydrocarbons, leaving simple compounds like carbon dioxide. It is essentially an extremely rapid oxidation process. By using the term blazing, the Lord is using an analogy for the fastest method of oxidation known to the people of Isaiah's day. Those of us who are chemists and researchers in this area look for ways to alter the oxidation process. It is through altered oxidation that one's teeth can be lightened, or that corrosion can be slowed. It is through slow oxidation that we age. If the aging process goes on long enough, what is living is oxidized to the point of becoming necrotic, or dead.

The above fire plague is expounded upon in Zechariah 14:12:

"This is the plague with which the Lord will strike all the nations that fought against Jerusalem: Their flesh will rot while they are still standing on their feet, their eyes will rot in their sockets, and their tongues will rot in their mouths."

For something to rot while one is on his feet, and before he can fall over—is sudden death indeed! In milliseconds then, living tissue will oxidize, rot, or become necrotic.

The author asks readers to bear with him while he relates a story that illustrates what happens with necrotic tissue.

When I was studying pathology at the Medical College of Georgia, we students had to examine organs from autopsies and conjecture about what had led to the person's demise. Prior to his death, one man being autopsied had been told by his physician not to do any exercise. He had suffered a heart attack, and was told that certain areas of the heart's tissues had to repair themselves before he could slowly begin any exercise program.

Instead of listening to the doctor, the patient decided to go jogging! As he was jogging, his heart began to build up pressure, and the area of the heart that had become necrotic simply gave way, causing his heart to explode like a balloon. This area had a consistency of cheese, and one could have easily put one's finger through it. I didn't even have to guess what had happened to the poor fellow. His heart had ruptured, due to caseous necrosis. The tissue had died and become very soft. When the extra pumping force from the good portion of his heart had exerted pressure above what the weak area could support, his heart literally exploded.

I haven't said all this just to be morbid, but in order to offer a clear picture of what will happen when the Lord inflicts the armies of opposition with mass necrosis.

For example, if the tissues in one's veins and arteries suddenly become necrotic, the internal blood pressure will cause the blood to burst out everywhere. It certainly would take a supernatural trigger to cause an instantaneous necrosis like this, but the physical result is very clear. One can only imagine the results of instant necrosis of the entire body.

The Bible reminds us that the secrets of the universe are held in the mind of Christ: *"Christ, in whom are hidden all the treasures of wisdom and knowledge"* (Col. 2:3). The word knowledge means science! He holds then, all the mysteries of science....but there is more. *"He is the image of the invisible God...For by him all things were created... He is before all things, and in him all things **hold** together"* (Col. 1:15-17).

*"The Son is the radiance of God's glory and the exact representation of his being, **sustaining** all things by his powerful word"* (Heb. 1:3).

Not only is Christ the possessor of all knowledge, and all science, but it is Christ who HOLDS or SUSTAINS all things together. He is then the power behind what we in science call the great nuclear binding force. It is Christ who keeps all those "+" plus charges of the protons in the nucleus together. They therefore don't repel from one another, causing things to come apart.

Since it is Christ that holds all things together, including the connective tissues of man, then it is a simple matter for Him to let go; producing instantaneous results.

Many people believe that this instantaneous necrosis will be caused by a nuclear explosion, such as a type of neutron bomb. But several things are wrong with this idea. An explosion of this type would not have the necessary surgical precision to remove evil weeds, without removing good wheat. Also, it is not plausible to think that God would allow man to displace Him of His just and rightful vengeance at this point and time, and to personally dispose of all His enemies. Rather, it is the End who generates the plague of plagues.

Let us take a final look, through the prophet Habakkuk, as he describes the Revelation of the Lord and associates the end time "plague" of Zechariah 14:12 with Him: *"His splendor was like the sunrise; rays flashed from his hand, where his power was hidden. Plague went before him"* (Hab. 3:4-5). Thus, the plague comes from the Lord, and not a neutron bomb.

GRAPES OF WRATH

The bodies of God's enemies will literally explode, and the blood will burst from their arteries and veins. It will be as it was predicted, like grapes when trampled, as described in Revelation 14:18-20. God's enemies have shed His own blood; now His long awaited vengeance will have arrived. Consider this chilling description by author Henry Morris, in, The Revelation Record:

"The bloodshed is so massive and so quick that the only apt comparison is the spurting of the juice from tremendous clusters of ripe fruit beneath the feet of the grape tramplers in a winepress. The hordes of civilians, many riding horses, no doubt many on foot, perhaps others on vehicles of one sort and another, thronging

194

together as in a great trough, unable to flee, their gaze transfixed on an amazing scene in the heavens, suddenly explode like bursting grapes, and the blood pours from a billion fountains."[56]

Since the horses and all the animals in the camps are stricken with this same "plague" of instantaneous necrosis (Zech. 14:14), the torrent of blood will drain to the valley where, as specifically prophesied, it will literally reach to the horse's bridles (Rev. 14:20)!

DARK HIGH NOON

We saw earlier that the coming of the Lord was with clouds of darkness (Psalm 18:9, 11). These clouds of darkness will cover up the sun, hiding people for protective purposes.

"'In that day,' declares the Sovereign Lord, 'I will make the sun go down at noon and darken the earth in broad daylight'" (Amos 8:9). God will also be answering the petition in the book of Isaiah:

"Make your shadow like night; at high noon. Hide the fugitives, do not betray the refugees" (Isa. 16:3).

END OF JEWISH JUDGEMENT

By this time, the Jews will have finished drinking from the cup of God's wrath (Isa. 51:22), and then it will be their enemies' turn (Isa. 51:23)! The Lord prepares to strike:

"O Lord, your hand is lifted high, but they do not see it. Let them see your zeal for your people and be put to shame; let the fire reserved for your enemies consume them" (Isa. 26:11).

---

[56] Tyndale House Publishers,Inc. Wheaton, Illinois; Creation-Life Publishers, San Diego, California, p. 276; used with permission.

The Lord reassures Israel that the fire will not harm them:

"When you pass through the waters, I will be with you; and when you pass through the rivers, they will not sweep over you. When you walk through the fire, you will not be burned; the flames will not set you ablaze" (Isa. 43:2).

The flames will be thick, but as Shadrach, Meshach, and Abednego found they were immune to the fiery furnace under the protection of the Son of God (the Messiah), so will the Israelites experience divine protection while her enemies are consumed.

"At the time of your appearing, you will make them like a fiery furnace. In his wrath the Lord will swallow them up, and his fire will consume them" (Psalm 21:9).

TURN ON THE LIGHTS—THE PARTY'S OVER

Again, it will be at noon on the end day—Yom Kippur—that the sun will go out. The stars will fall from the sky (Matt. 24:29; Isa. 13:10; 34:4). As the heavens tremble, the earth will shake from its place (Isa. 13:13).[57]

At evening time, when darkness normally falls, the light comes on—man's 6,000 year "party" of rebellion is over.

"When evening comes, there will be light" (Zech. 14:7).

The whole world will see light that many man-made nuclear explosions couldn't even begin to touch.

"His lightning lights up the world; the earth sees and trembles. The mountains melt like wax before the Lord, before the Lord of all the earth" (Psalm 97:4-5).

---

[57] This may be the earth tilting on its axis, as well as quaking, which will also prevent having dark winters at the earth's icy poles during the Millennial Day.

When the light of God is revealed, His enemies will flee like cockroaches. When the great earthquake strikes, it will be more damaging than all previous earthquakes in mankind's history (Rev. 16:18). Great hail stones will be generated by the collapsing mountains and the resulting volcanic explosions.

"From the sky huge hailstones of about a hundred pounds each fell upon men. And they cursed God on account of the plague of hail, because the plague was so terrible" (Rev. 16:21).

The giant hailstones will produce intense cyclic waves of altering atmospheric high and low pressures, creating great vacuums. Simultaneously, those who have been struck with the instantaneous necrosis plague will create a river of blood as their blood vessels will be vacuumed dry. It will be a terrible and fearful day indeed, but the prayer of the psalmist will have been answered, *"Let burning coals fall upon them; may they be thrown into the fire, into miry pits, never to rise"* (Psalm 140:10).

As in the days of old, the armies of these anti-Christian anti-Semitists will be struck supernaturally with madness (Zech. 12:4) and blindness (Zeph. 1:17), even before the Lord's fire and sword is called upon.

"For with fire and with his sword the Lord will execute judgement upon all men, and many will be those slain by the Lord" (Isa. 66:16).

The flesh of kings, generals, and great and small men alike (Rev. 19:18) will have been prepared as the great and terrible "supper" of God, upon which the fowls of the air will gorge themselves.

Man's "week" of doing things his way, will have come to THE END!

SUMMARY

The nations, along with the Antichrist, are led to Jerusalem by different forces. The city is captured, the houses ransacked, and the women raped (Zech. 14:2).

Cosmic disturbances appear everywhere. As the Omega approaches the earth, the mountains and hills begin to melt, and the earth and man begins to shake. Mountains and islands disappear. Earthquakes, volcanic upheavals, thunderstorms, lightning, and tidal waves wreak terror. At 12:00 noon, the light goes out as the Lion of God, with flames in His eyes, comes in thick darkness to take His long awaited vengeance. At evening, the glory of God with unbelievable light appears. The Antichrist is bound by Jesus' brightness, snatched up alive, and escorted by angels at unseen speed to the Lake of Fire, while the world's armies look on. The vast armies then begin to flee as the Jews begin to chase. As in the battles of old, supernatural beings and elements are employed. Mighty men, kings, generals, and all the people who were gathered against Jerusalem will flee; their bodies explode with their own blood, like grapes being trampled. Countless vultures excitedly fly overhead, and contemplate a feast such as they have never imagined.

It all ends very quickly!

EPILOGUE

Those who see God as the Father of all and only as a God of love cannot help but be troubled deeply at the above scenes. Almighty Creator God, the Alpha, must one day become the Omega and bring this age to its end. God is not just a God of love, but a holy God who demands justice. God's justice demands that He judges sin and all its consequences. He is equally the Alpha and the Omega. By His sovereign will He created all things, and by the same sovereign will, only He can bring all things to consummation. May our admonition be that of the Apostle in 2 Peter 1:19 (paraphrased): *"May we more reverently search the more sure Word of prophecy, and pay attention to it—as to a light shining in a dark place, until the Millennial Day dawns."*

As we search God's Word, there are still many details to put together *("we see through a glass, darkly")*. For those of us who have bowed our knee to Christ, the deepest of gratitude should be ours. For as we see the sun setting, and the dark night of the end drawing closer, we have the hope and the promise of Omega Himself, that He, *"...will rescue us from the coming wrath"* (1 Thess. 1:10). All who have this hope of His appearing should be led to purify themselves, *"...just as he is pure"* (1 John 3:3).

There should also be a tangible fear in those whose hope is not based on Jesus Christ. They would be wise to come to Him while they can—to His cross, where the fire and wrath have already burned, where there is eternal protection from all future judgements. Serious indeed is the issue at stake—it is eternal damnation or everlasting life! We have to decide in this life where we will spend eternity. To choose to do nothing is in itself a disastrous decision. Since we must consciously choose Christ in order to be saved, our non-choice is no less a conscious choice for eternal damnation in the Lake of Fire.

Unfortunately, the end will be "THE END" for most, for "...*broad is the road that leads to destruction*" (*Matt. 7:13*). On the other hand, for those whose hope is based on Jesus Christ, The End is really only The Beginning!

AN INVITATION FROM THE AUTHOR

The Spirit of God closes His Book of prophecy, the Bible, with an invitation: *"The Spirit and the bride say, `Come!' and let him who hears say, 'Come!' Whoever is thirsty, let him come; and whoever wishes, let him take the free gift of the water of life"* (Rev. 22:17).

Although there is no comparison between my humble book and God's, I feel that I should follow this pattern, and close mine in like manner. I would like to begin with two passages from the Bible, each in the form of a question:

"How shall we escape if we ignore such a great salvation" (Heb. 2:3)?

"See to it that you do not refuse him who speaks. If they did not escape when they refused him who warned them on earth, how much less will we, if we turn away from him who warns us from heaven" (Heb. 12:25)?

A permanent escape from God's fiery judgement and indignation has been provided. He poured out His wrath on His Son, Messiah "Ben Joseph"—who was humanity's Passover Lamb, the sacrifice for all of us (Heb. 9:28). God did this so He would not have to pour out His wrath on us. His sole condition, our part, is that we accept Christ's sacrificial death upon the cross as forgiveness for our sins. Thousands of already fulfilled prophecies give us assurance that we can believe everything the Bible tells us.

The Bible states:

"You must be born again" (John 3:7)—

That the new birth or salvation is only in Jesus Christ, *"Salvation is found in no one else, for there is no other name under heaven given to men by which we must be saved"* (Acts 4:12)—

That it applies to all people, *"...that everyone who believes in him may have eternal life. For God so loved the* world that he gave his one and only Son, that whoever believes in him shall not perish but have eternal life" (John 3:15, 16)—

And that salvation is only a prayer away, "*That if you confess with your mouth, 'Jesus is Lord,' and believe in your heart that God raised Him from the dead, you will be saved. Everyone who calls on the name of the Lord will be saved*" (Rom. 10:9, 13).

Is there any reason to procrastinate?

"*Today, if you hear his voice, do not harden your hearts*" (Heb. 3:7-8, 15; 4:7).

Accept God's gift of escape NOW, rather than His judgement later, by repeating this sinner's prayer and believing it in your heart:

"*Lord, I haven't known you or had a relationship with you. I was blind, but now I see. I want to escape your wrath. I believe that you have paid the price for my sins at your cross, by the sacrifice of your only Son. I confess with my mouth that Jesus is Lord, and I believe in my heart that You raised Him from the dead. Thus, I am saved. THANK YOU for saving me! Amen.*"

Congratulations are in the highest order if you have just accepted the Lord! Not only do you escape the coming wrath, but the wrath you would have received if you would have died before receiving Christ as Lord. That is, you have now escaped the penalty for your past sins, which would have meant going to hell when you die. That in itself is enough reason to rejoice! But there is more good news. You now have power over your present sins—doing your will when it is contrary to God's. As you exercise this new prerogative, you will enjoy the abundant life of Christ, instead of the wanton, empty life of this world. You will soon be removed completely from the presence of sin, either by rapture or death, then to begin eternal life with our Creator and Consummator—Jesus Christ.

You'll more clearly see that you have escaped, as you sin less and less each day and begin to receive and experience the abundant life here on earth—a life that has brand new meaning and purpose. The things of this world that you once desired so much will begin to be replaced by the desires of your new Father in heaven. Ask Him now to lead and guide you from now until the end of your days—or until the end of the age, whichever comes first.

People everywhere should be reminded of the closing words of Jesus, the Alpha and the Omega: *"Yes, I am coming soon"* (Rev. 22:20). For you, whose wisdom has exceeded your pride, and who have humbled yourself unto salvation, may you not fear but rejoice over

THE END.

"The grace of the Lord Jesus be with God's people. Amen"

Revelation 22:21.

TIMELINE

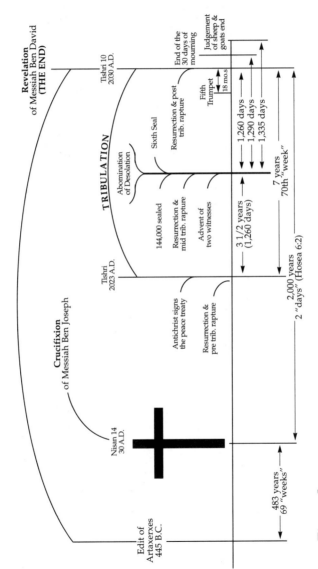

Figure I

205

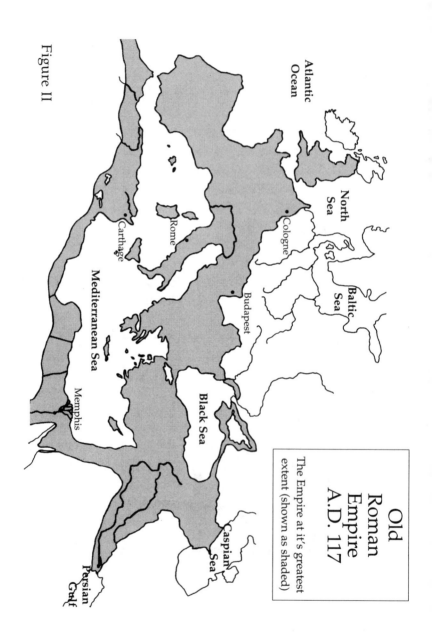

Figure II

Atlantic
Ocean

North
Sea

Baltic
Sea

Cologne

Budapest

Carthage

Rome

Mediterranean Sea

Memphis

Black Sea

Caspian
Sea

Persian
Gulf

Old
Roman
Empire
A.D. 117

The Empire at it's greatest
extent (shown as shaded)

206

To view or download the book from
the Internet, visit my website:
http://www.theend.org

To make a comment,
please e-mail me at:
gmadray@theend.org

REVIEWS

"You are, obviously, a scholar. Your work is comprehensive and thorough...."

Carole Carlson
Co-author of *The Late Great Planet Earth*
Solvang, CA

"As a writer of some 37 Biblical textbooks, I can highly recommend the reading of Dr. George Madray's Biblical book of these end times. These writings reveal a tremendous amount of research and study, by a man of God who has been called of God for this particular work of revealing combined facts of the end of the age. As a professional Doctor, he has gone that extra mile to use his talents to glorify God. It is of the utmost necessity that Christians of today study this informative book, of the things of tomorrow."

Rev. Dr. Andrew J. Losier
Founder and President
Christian Literature & Bible Center Inc.
Toccoa, GA

"In the years that I have known Dr. Madray, he has had a heart for spreading the gospel, and an analytical mind toward the word of God. Everyone can see as we are approaching the new millennium, we all would be wise in studying Dr. Madray's works concerning the end times, and prophecy.

Dr. Greg Pierce, Thd.DM.DB
Lee County, VA